BECOMING

A

CONQUEROR

How to Keep the Past from Invading Your Present and Destroying Your Future

Dr. GeGe Jasmin

Legacy Publishing
Imagination at Work

www.legacypublishing.us

Becoming a Conqueror: How to Keep the Past
from Invading Your Present and Destroying Your Future
ISBN: 978-1-94463-200-7
LCCN: 2019945745

Dedication

This book is dedicated to my husband Mr. Ronel Jasmin, who through his strength and unbiased support I have been able to come this far.

ACKNOWLEDGMENT

I will remain forever grateful to Almighty God for his unending grace, through the sufficient light from His word "The Scripture" on my path I have been guided into making this idea and dream a reality. The prayers of my family members cannot be over - emphasized.

This work would not have seen the light of the day if not for the prayers, guides, and support of people like my husband Mr. Ronel Jasmin, My son Ronny Jasmin and my daughters Zelene and Zariah Jasmin respectively. Also, I am not forgetting the support from my brother Junior Ormilus, and I thank my mother Princess Bastien for her constant encouragement.

Thanks too to my friends and well-wishers, may God continue to bless you all.

Table of Contents

INTRODUCTION

"I can do all things through Christ who
strengthens me"

Philippians 4:13

This verse sounds so empowering. We, as
Christians love saying it, it makes us feel good for
one reason or another, if only at least for a moment.

Most of us have memorized it hoping that if
we repeat it often enough, it will manifest itself and
fill up all the blank spaces and answer all the
question marks in our lives. However, we are
perplexed when our lives do not reflect all the
things we can do through His strength.

Why is that?

We teach our children this verse as early as
possible to ingrain the truth into them that the
possibilities are endless with God on our side. Yet,
our daily living and practice seem to be speaking a
different story.

Why?

That is the precise question I asked myself fourteen years ago: "If I can do all things through Christ who strengthens me, why is the gap between what I am doing and what I can do so wide? Why is it that I am constantly fighting to do what I know I can do?

I know that I have been blessed beyond measures. Having the opportunity to live and raise a family in this beautiful country wow me all the time. Looking from the outside, life seems magical. So, why do I feel that I've short- changed the God who makes everything possible by failing to do everything that I am capable of.

Every time I want to reach for the stars, there is always something, often in the form of someone, an obstacle, a memory, a situation, thrusting me in the midst of turbulent psychological and emotional chaos reminding me sometimes in what appears to be the most caring and loving ways to, "Don't even think about it, how can you in good conscience write this book when you're still such a big mess? Wow! What will people think of you? Come on! Stop being a hypocrite."

For fourteen years I listened to that voice telling me that I am not good enough and the best thing to do is to shut my mouth or I will be exposed for the fraud that I am. So, I brought into this mindset. I gave into fear. I became timid. I talked only when I had to. I did not go for the dreams that God placed upon my heart. I decided to listen to the enemy instead of grabbing and holding tight to the promises of God.

But, God does not give up on his children and when he gives you a gift, no one can take it away from you. It was during one of my morning Bible study that God placed the burden in my heart to write this book: "Becoming a Conqueror: How to Keep the Past from Invading your Present and Destroying your Future".

It was a custom for me during that time to take a walk after completing my studies. The title was given to me so clearly and after all these years, there is no mistake on what the Lord was trying to teach me.

I fully recognized and understood at the time that I was in the middle of a battle. I realized that the enemy used my past to paralyze me with fear, doubt and to render me useless from accomplishing the work of the Kingdom of my Heavenly Father.

Yet to stand strong to acknowledge the enemy and conquer these tactics that were constantly being used against me seemed to be impossible. So, day after day, year after year, the evidence of progress was sporadic.

So, the Spirit of God is constantly bringing the book into my mind and many efforts have been made … this book may have been written at least five times, the drafts menacingly reminded me of the many negative consequences that I stand to endure if I were to publish them.

What threats?

I often ponder on what people will say and how my family and friends would ostracize me. The majority of them would rather sweep everything under the rug and continue to paint the pretense of the perfect family.

The thoughts kept coming and they brought me to (Romans: 8:37) which declares that "I am more than a conqueror through Christ who loved me". I grabbed on to the word "conqueror" because too often I felt I was in a battle. I was fighting for my very existence and being a conqueror meant that I had the tools to win the battle at hand. As a matter of fact, Jesus declared that the battle is already won.

The truth is we live in a broken world. Daily, we experience violence, divorce, crimes, financial difficulties, natural disasters, and diseases that ravage all aspects of our lives. Every single one of us has been touched by the ever-reaching cycle of sin, threatening every day to consume and destroy our lives.

But it is not over. God is here and will always be here to take care of his children, to uphold and strengthen us, and to build and to finish the good work He started in us. In this process, we become conquerors, who keep the past from invading our present and destroying our futures.

We tend to be so afraid of the future because of what we have experienced in the past – disappointments, abuse, betrayal, loss, tragedies of every kind, etc. That, in turn, becomes the precedence of how we live from moment-to-moment. We no longer have to allow this invasion to take over our lives, we can walk in victory because the battle is already won.

<u>Introduction Notes</u>

_____

_____

_____

_____

_____

_____

_____

_____

_____

_____

_____

_____

_____

_____

_____

_____

_____

_____

_____

_____

_____

_____

<u>Work It Out</u>

Memorize:

Philippians 4:13

"I can do all things through Christ who strengthens me."

Journal:

Prompt:

How have you understood Philippians 4:13 to work in your life? How have you implemented this verse into your life? Are you satisfied? Where do you see you can make an improvement to take full advantage of this verse?

Pray:

Lord, help me to completely believe that I can do all things through you, amen.

Quote to Ponder:

"God does not give up on his children

and when he gives you a gift, no one

can take it away from you."

Chapter 1

A Living Miracle

"There are only two ways to live your life.
One is as though nothing is a miracle,
The other is as though everything is a
miracle."
— *Albert Einstein*

It was a dark night and the storm raged on top of my grandfather, myself, and the donkey that was leading the way. The lightning increased with every step giving us short glimpses of the trees standing their grounds on both sides of us.

I wanted to hold my grandfather's hand but he assured me that walking in the middle was best in case any dangerous situations presented themselves. I cried incessantly while my grandfather encouraged my every step on the way.

Although this was one of the scariest moments of my life, it is also one that I treasure the most. Up until this day, my extended family would tell me that I was grandpa's favorite. He would take me with him whenever he could to make sure that I was well taken care of.

This was not a customary thing for a man to do in the countryside of Jacmel, Haiti in the late seventies, where we lived. Somehow, he felt a special connection to me because he loved my mother so much. I want to venture to say that he felt a special connection to me because somehow he felt responsible for what happened to my mother.

You see my grandfather and my grandmother had ten children and my mother was the sixth child. Like so many of her older siblings, when my mother was about twelve or thirteen years old, she was sent to Port-au-Prince, the capital city of Haiti to serve as a domestic to one of grandma's friends.

Poor families all around Haiti practice this in order to help ease the burden of taking care of a big family in a land where providing food is an everyday challenge. So, this detestable practice allows the domestic child to work for pennies around the clock in exchange for food and shelter.

As if often as the case, my mother, vulnerable and unprotected in a strange city, got pregnant. My soon-to-be grandmother challenged the fact that my mother was indeed pregnant for one of her sons. She immediately organized transportation for my mother to go back to Jacmel to her parents all alone and without any aid whatsoever.

Neighbors pitied her and offered my mother a beer and some pills to get rid of the baby. A thirteen-year-old girl had no business having a baby in this already difficult world. God spoke to her heart, she decided not to follow through with the directions she was given.

My maternal grandfather vowed to chop my father's head off if he ever laid eyes on him, so I spent the first few years with my mother since Haitian mothers are known to breastfeed their babies for a long time. My mother claimed to have breastfed me for two years. Upon my weaning off the breast, she went back to the city to look for work. She came back from time to time to bring supplies, but very few memories of her during those years remained, but memories with my grandfather abound. Our time together was something special as we did almost everything together.

It was not all great times. I particularly remember being left alone for long periods of time without care and experiencing the ping of hunger. I vividly remembered the twist and turn of my stomach one day and I searched the yard for any fruit that may have fallen from a tree. I found a cantaloupe like fruit Haitians called "Abrico."

This particular fruit must be peeled the right way or the aftermath of eating this fruit could be disastrous. Although I knew that at about four or five years old, I did a novice job in preparing this fruit, so the result was a stomach ache the like I have never known. I suffered alone for what seemed to be an eternity.

No, it was not all great times. I had a problem with wetting the bed. My grandfather and I slept on what we call "nat," our own version of the rug made out of dried banana and plantain leaves.

We would place the few sheets that we had over the rug like structure to go to sleep on daily. Night after night I would wet the bed.

In the morning, I was responsible to dry them in the sun for the next night. The only spanking I ever received from my grandfather was the result of me not carrying out that responsibility. After so many days and weeks of sleeping on these bacteria infested rug and sheets, my skin broke out in rashes and boils all over my body. Getting rid of them was no easy task. My grandmother boiled leaves of all kinds for a special bath. This bath left me trembling with blood running all over my body as these boils were purged and rubbed vigorously with a handful of leaves.

When I was about nine years old, my mother sent for me. By this time, she had a new boyfriend and a new son, we were five years apart. Her boyfriend made it clear that I was not welcomed in his home and numerous arguments resulted from my presence.

These arguments would often lead to fights where I would find myself frantically screaming for help to rescue my mother. My mother could not afford to send me to a Catholic school like my brother, so she sent me to a neighborhood school, my first recollection of being taught in a group of students my age. In Jacmel, once in a blue moon, a visiting teacher showed up to give us all lessons, adults, and children of all ages simultaneously.

Despite the many fights and the uncomfortable living conditions, I learned quickly. I learned games from the neighborhood children, entertaining the older folks with new songs and dances, helping my mother at the marketplace, starting my first business, and learning how to braid hair. However, during that time, I became vulnerable in a different way.

Trusted family friends would often ask my mother for me to run errands for them. I remember three specific men who often requested that I go somewhere with them or to go buy and bring them something. The result would be time alone with them, where they would touch me inappropriately. Although I felt violated, the fear of accusing a grown-up was unheard of. In addition, I did not know what all of the inappropriate touching and kissing were about. My mother and I have never had a conversation about sex or how to protect myself as a young lady. So, I never said anything.

When I was about ten years old, my father's cousin got my mother and my father reconnected. They started communicating via letters and voice recordings. My father was now living in New York and was interested in bringing me to live with him in the states. My mother was ecstatic about this proposition because it was an opportunity for me to create a better life.

So, at eleven years old, I met my father and we bonded quickly because I was an inquisitive and helpful child. During that meeting, I learned that I had another brother from my father with a different woman. My new brother made it to New York before me, because my father was more involved in his life from birth, so fewer official documents had to be redone.

Leaving my mom and my little brother, who had become my world was excruciatingly painful since this was the closest to a family life I have ever had. Upon reaching New York, I met my father for a second time and his new wife. She was beautiful and welcoming and good to us, my new brother and I.

My stepmother was learning to become a cosmetologist, had a home salon where she did the hair of the women around town. As in my nature, I was right by her side passing her rollers, pins, and cleaning after her. Even though we shared a one-bedroom for the four of us, she kept the apartment and us immaculate. However, less than six months later, she was gone. My father was sneaky when it comes to beating his wife, he locked her in closets and bathrooms to minimize the noise. But, one day when he assumed we were sleeping I witnessed one of their fights. He held a knife on her insisting that she tells him about her affair. I felt afraid, so I did not dare to say anything.

After her departure, our condition of life deteriorated. I took more responsibility with the cooking and cleaning as well as taking care of my own self like doing my hair and dressing myself. It was hilarious how I dressed in her clothes and style my hair like she styled hers.

During that time three more people moved into the one-bedroom apartment – my paternal grandmother, my aunt, and a much older cousin. That is when I ended up sleeping on a twin bed with my father. I thought I was having a nightmare. I felt like someone was suffocating me in my sleep. I awoke to find my father's mouth all over my face. Fear paralyzed me, so I did not move.

We moved to Miami less than two years of my arrival to New York, where I met an uncle who had a soccer team for a family. I counted twelve. We were to stay with them until we can get our own home. The molestation and abuse diminished to a great extent due to the sheer number of people in the house.

By some miracle, my stepmother traveled later to be with us and it was apparent that she and my father had made up. For some reason, I became very sad and depressed. They could not find the reason for my sadness, so they try to beat it out of me. That did not work and my relationship with my stepmother became strained.

We moved to a three-bedroom home in Hollywood, Florida with an in-ground pool in the backyard and a huge billiard table in the family room. It was the biggest place we've ever called our home and I hoped desperately to be safe in my room.

Indeed, I was safe for about a year. Once again, my father and wife's relationship deteriorated with arguments that led to physical abuse. My father had a master bedroom with a walk-in closet now, so he conducted most of his beatings in there, out of our site.

One particular evening, we heard screaming coming from their room, so my brother and I pleaded to him to let her go. She was a very fair skin lady, so he pounded on her in areas she could cover, but this time, I saw the purple bruises on her arms and clumps of hair missing in areas once full. We were dumb and mute; we would not dare to say or do anything.

The abuse escalated. He sneaked his way to my room late at night. I was scared to death and cried hysterically most nights. Upon their second break up, my brother and I were sent to live with a cousin and her family in Orlando, Florida. There were a total of seven children not to include her husband, and her mother. My brother and I added two to make eleven in the house.

They were good to us. No abuse for a whole year, what a blessing. I blossomed in my own way – styling my cousins' hair, excelling at school, and finding and keeping a job to help pay for our personal needs. I got cozy with an older boy and when my father learned about it, he slapped and beat me with a log. Then he proceeded to use the words in the Bible to instruct me on how a modest and God fearing young lady is supposed to behave.

The vibrant extrovert of a child I once were has disappeared the moment I set foot in this country. The duplicity of pretending to be Christians while committing acts the heathens would never imagine translated into a sense of shame and guilt that continues to be a struggle.

To make matters worse, my sole purpose became to protect my father's reputation regardless of what he was doing to me. He was in the ministry, leading the flock on the weekends. I thought I was doing the Lord's work by making my father my best friend, forgiving him often, and using everything in my power to help him in any way that he needed.

Looking back, I realize that I did not have the tools or the strength to conquer him, so I gave up and settled into this inferiority complex, shame, guilt, and thought that I was damaged beyond repair.

I did not have the sufficient language to express myself or the psychological skills to deal with what was happening to me. In the first place, our culture did not permit the voices of children to be heard because they were not allowed to question adult behavior.

Secondly, my father was an expert in hiding his true self and most people adored him. He was such a good pretender that everybody was convinced of what a good Christian and family man he was.

Finally, there seemed to be no one I could trust, no one I could talk to, so I kept the abuse secretly to myself. I was totally confused because my father was a Christian, and he was offered leadership positions wherever he went. This was the beginning of my religious doubts, and I started questioning God's existence. If God did exist why would He allow one of His own to have such abhorrent behaviors?

Many people go through these kind of experiences and are forever affected and changed by them. At the beginning, I tried to block these things out of my mind I hoped that if I pretended that nothing was happening, I would wake up from the nightmare. But this never happened and, on the contrary, things continued to get worse.

In my childish mind I could only try to find out what I had done to deserve such a treatment and suffering. I started to doubt if God was really watching over me or not. I started to suspect that religion was just one big lie to keep us in ignorance and slavery.

How could God allow such terrible things to take place in the world? If there really was a God, did the existence of so such evil mean that He was actually a malicious and careless God?

That question remained unanswered for many long and hard years. Doubt, indecision, fear, and a poor self-image plagued me for a long period of my life, and I was constantly imprisoned between opposite thoughts. I was so troubled that I tried to take my life several times.

However, in the midst of this darkness, God planted a seed inside me that rendered me unable to cause major or permanent damage to myself. As a result, I did not like God very much. I thought he was manipulating and sabotaging me, just like my father had done for so many years. Why didn't He allow me to go through with it? So, I prayed what I thought would be my last prayer.

"Lord, I cannot take this anymore. Where are you? Don't you see what is happening to me? I am tired. This is no way to live a life. What is the point anyway? This time, I am going to get it done the right way. I am going to make sure of it. If you do exist, show yourself. Do something!"

Because I was right at my breaking point, I made this last appeal. God answered my prayer and in His wisdom, He sent me my husband. I did not expect "a husband" by that time; that was the last thing I had in my mind when I requested Him to "do something".

Only when I could see things in retrospective, did I come to understand why God had answered my prayer the way He did. The truth is that most of the times, God answers our prayers in ways we do not comprehend at the precise moment.

When I decided to speak light into the darkness, I was pictured as the evil one, the liar, and the divisive one. God knew I needed help to stand strong and not to give up. I also learned that God had always been there in my troubles and had communicated with me.

Remember, he planted his Word into my heart and I could not get away from Him. However, I still did not trust Him by that time. The picture I had of God was not appealing, and I refused to obey Him because of my unbelief.

Despite all of this, I had some good things going on. I enjoyed reading and often the discrepancies between what I learned from the books and the reality of my life forced me to become aware of the complexity of my situation and asked my abuser many questions. I cherished learning about people's lives, how they overcome obstacles, and how they became successful. Along the way, I carried a huge responsibility to become successful in order to provide for the family that I left in Haiti. This was not something I put on myself, this was something that was expected.

Therefore, I took my education seriously and took every opportunity I had to go to summer school from middle school to the university level. My teachers told me that education was the way, so I studied and earned many degrees without a sense of direction.

Looking back, it was my greatest coping mechanism. What I really wanted to study, I did not have the confidence to go for it. For as longs as I can remember, I was singing, dancing, acting, writing, and making people laugh. Regardless of this deep sense of awareness of how all of these things were affecting me, I worked very hard at keeping my true self from the world.

But so many people, books, sermons, songs, stories, and observations got in the way and forced me to look at life differently. They are a constant reminder that I have not only the choice but the tools to conquer these inadequacies.

However, the problems remained because I could not get away from my father; I felt responsible for him. My pleas that he should allow me to leave, to learn to live on my own and follow my own dreams were dropped on deaf ears, so the great manipulator would find a way to make me do whatever he wanted, often quoting Biblical passages, faking sickness, or even pain.

In my gullibility and naivety, I failed to connect along the way how he worked diligently to sabotage all of the relationships that he felt threatened by. I learned this well into my adulthood when I desperately wanted to get away and felt trapped in my own home.

I thought and planned my suicide a number of times, my weak faith in my fragile relationship with Jesus kept me alive, because I needed to go to Heaven, the paradise where I would be whole for real. So, I never developed the guts to go all the way.

I could not do it on my own. I needed help to get away from my father. The opportunity presented itself through someone I knew in my teens. We attended the same Church when I lived in Hollywood, Florida; we had crushes on each other. I was fourteen and he was sixteen.

This was one potential relationship that my father crushed - he knew that we liked each other by recording every phone call that came through the house. He came back into my life more than twelve years later, but this time, he was divorced with three children.

We immediately bonded, but I thought our time had passed. I needed help not more problems. What would people say? What would my mother say? What would my brothers say? They looked up to me and did not realize that I needed more help than they did. I could not keep up with all of the expectations of my life. I needed a change and this seemed like my best chance.

He was the only man who did not cower in the presence of my father. He remained focused on his goal not to give up this time. Things got really crazy and strange things started happening when I decided that I would marry him. I find myself simultaneously in a whirlwind of my father's most complicated schemes, a greater sense of my insecurities, court battles, and a brand new family I had no clue how to manage.

The invasion took on a higher dimension, I was afraid and depressed and it showed. I would spend weeks without getting up from the couch to take care of myself or anyone else. My new husband could not understand why it was so hard for me to make decisions when it came to dealing with my father and why I find it difficult to take his side on certain matters, so we started arguing.

In the meantime, we had three additions to the family in the first two years of our marriage. We added to each other's pain and soon realized that this was not easier than before. We both experienced tremendous obstacles and harbored unresolved pain that crept into our arguments.

It was about one year into our marriage that I decided to tell my husband about the abuse and gave him the option to leave this relationship if it was too much for him to bear. We had a son together and I knew giving him this news now was not fair to him.

I did not want to create another prison for myself and decided to risk destroying this new marriage and complicate the future of our son. He decided to stay.

As the battle rage on, I added more hurts, hang-ups, disappointments with life and career, poor decisions, identity crisis, loss of loved ones, and financial disaster that led to a reluctant bankruptcy.

Throughout these times of my life, I felt a sense of paralysis because I had big goals and dreams.

Frequently, the past insecurities invade my present moments to remind me that I am damaged goods; therefore, not good enough to make a significant contribution to the world, even if it is just being comfortable in my own skin.

The present continues to be spoiled by irrational and negative self-talk and thoughts. Although I knew that creating my future depended on the decisions I made in my present, I still could not carry it through to longevity.

My healing journey started with four books: "Lord Heal My Hurts" by Kay Arthur, "Bad Childhood, Good Life" by Dr. Laura Schlessinger, "The Battlefield of the Mind" by Joyce Meyer, and The Success Principle: "How to Get from Where You Are to Where You Want to Be" by Jack Canfield.

Along with the Bible, these books helped to purge my soul, to take responsibility for my life, and to gain a new understanding of the battle that I constantly fight. It has been an ongoing journey and now I want to share with you what I have learned along the way that has equipped me to keep the past from invading my present and destroying my future.

My hope is to help equip you to do the same.

Quote to Ponder:

"He planted his Word into my heart

and I could not get away

from Him."

Chapter Notes

_____

_____

_____

_____

_____

_____

_____

_____

_____

_____

_____

_____

_____

_____

_____

_____

_____

_____

_____

_____

_____

_____

_____

<u>Work It Out</u>

Memorize:

Romans 8: 28

"…all things work together for good to those who love God, to those who are called according to his purpose".

Journal:

Prompt:

How is your life a miracle? What is your story? Write it out completely.

Pray:

Lord, help me use my story to help people become conquerors to confront their pasts and secure a bright future. Amen.

Chapter 2

A Broken Life, A Broken World

"For everyone has sinned;
we all fall short of God's glorious standard".
Romans 3:23

Is your life broken? Are you constantly being invaded by negative images of your past? Do you feel overwhelmed by them? You are not alone. The whole world is broken and seems to be falling apart.

It is not hard to see it. Whenever you turn on your television, radio, or computer on, the negative stories far outnumber the positive ones. The terrible real-life stories about murder, corruption, abuse, divorce, robbery, war, terrorism, drugs, and hunger are all over the different media.

No, you don't have to look hard or far to see that you are living in a broken world. We are all affected. We are all one. The same way one person's action on the other side of the world affects you, what you do has the potential to affect others around or even far from you.

We all have a past we are not proud of or a history of brokenness—a history of the constant invasion of our minds and hearts. That has been so since Adam and Eve decided to listen to the Serpent in the garden instead of listening to God. We are all guilty. We have done bad things to others and others have done bad things to us. That is the spiral effect of sin.

But God is waiting for you with open arms. It may be hard for you to see a loving God in the midst of your pain. I understand. I've been there. I know just what you are thinking about and can empathize with you on this part of your life. I went through it too, had the same feelings, and know what you will go through after you read these words I have written.

This is because my experience is the common and ever repeating experience of all of us, but it will be recognized as such only if you are willing to fully understand.

"God, why are you letting this happen to me? Don't you love me? What did I do to deserve this?" For many years, I kept asking God the same questions over and over again. I could not understand why He would allow sexual abuse on a small child.

I did not understand why my father could commit such a sin and still maintain his position as a leader in our church. Seeing how good he was at deceiving people and apparently going on with his life with total immunity, I felt I had no other way out but to commit suicide.

There was an inner battle waging inside me. I did not want to hurt the one who had turned my life upside down though. I seriously thought he was disturbed. How else could I explain this?

What is more, I did not want to harm those who thought so highly of him and the gospel he preached either. So I kept it all to myself, hoping that one day I would have the courage to take my own life. I was disturbed. I was disturbed by the absence of God in my life and, at the same time, so disturbed that I was unable to recognize the real causes of my disturbance.

Needless to say God did not permit that to happen. Despite the tremendous misuse of the Word of God in the greater portion of my life, God saw it good and appropriate to plant his seeds into my heart. He kept me yearning for his Word.

As a result, I wanted to read and understand His Word through the leading of the Holy Spirit. That was when He led me to the book of Jeremiah, where I learned that we are being invaded by our pasts and sins because we have turned away from God. Jeremiah 2: verse 17 and 18 states:

And you have brought this upon yourselves by rebelling against the Lord your God, even though He was leading you on the way. Your wickedness will bring its own punishment. Your turning from me will shame you. You will see what an evil, bitter thing it is to abandon the Lord Your God and not to fear Him.

This is truly the act of a magnificent God who can forgive His followers for the greatest of their sins and for having been absent from His present for any short or long period of time. But God understands human nature; after all He created it and implanted it within each of us.

Therefore, anything that man has created is also the work of God and should be revered as such. Self-pleasure must be turned against its origins rather than focused internally.

That means we are seeking to please ourselves rather than to please God. We have created materialism, money, social position, careers and false idols. We have given our precious time to television, the Internet, and to electronic toys instead of giving our time to God.

We seem to have time to spend on anything, but not to dedicate to God. We have forgotten what God has done for us. We are reluctant to remember what God has done for us as an excuse to continue our wayward ways.

In this broken world, we are encouraged to remain in our steady situations. We are kept trapped not only by the intrusions from the past but also from external forces. On a daily basis, we are subjected to a barrage of messages that undermine our self-consciousness and destroy any values that we may have created within ourselves.

We see the lifestyles of the rich and famous presented not only as attainable desires, see them as admirable figures to follow, but also see their lives as lives we would love to live ourselves and see all the things they do as activities we would like to engage in, such as social events, crazy parties, traveling, driving fast cars and maintaining an overall frantic life. The media relays this information in an unquestionable manner urging us onwards to this path of material consumption.

We are expected to compare ourselves with these popular icons in every aspect of our lives. Rather than questioning the validity of these imagery and these lifestyles; we tend to question ourselves. We consider that it must be us who are broken or mistaken rather than the world around us. We start to look for answers to questions that do not actually exist. If we are asking the wrong questions in the wrong places, how can we expect to find the truth?

Instead of letting God into our lives, these modern and praised diversions push Him to the fringes and He becomes more and more distant from us, precisely in those times when we most need Him. In these moments, to pull God back into the center of our world may seem impossible at first.

This is because of the harm and pain that we have carried with us for so long and that has clouded our vision. Everything is seen through the lenses of our past and our reality has become skewed.

You are probably suffering for a different reason than I am. We all have different life stories, however, suffering is always the same emotion. You may have inflicted your own wounds or others may have caused you pain.

You may suffer from constant thoughts of worthlessness and dirtiness. You may be plagued by memories you wish would go away. It does not matter what caused your pain. Pain is pain, and it hurts.

Please, understand that I am not being insensitive to your pain. I've been there, so I know how you feel. When you turn away from God, one sin begets another and another.

The story of David, which can be found in 2 Samuel 11, illustrates that point very well. Lusting after Bathsheba, Uriah's wife tempted David. He did not resist the temptation; instead, he welcomed it by summoning and sleeping with her. He deceived others and deliberately committed murder by killing Uriah to cover up his sins.

When we get started in sin, it is difficult to stop as James 1:14 relates. We get trapped in a dangerous net we cannot escape from on our own. As stated earlier, I did not want people to know I was abused. Instead of turning to God and cry: "Oh Lord, if You heal me, I will be truly healed; if You save me, I will be truly saved, my praises are for You alone" (Jeremiah 17:14).

I lied, committed sins against my body, and attempted suicide a number of times. So, as you can see, the sins continue to get bigger until they get to completely and disastrously invade our lives. Then, we become blind regarding where we should go or what we should do.

When we turn our backs on God and sin, we are not the only ones who suffer the consequences of that. Our families, communities, our country, and even the entire world will suffer the impact of our disobedience.

They are all being invaded. They are all being damaged because we have sinned against God and against each other. But we don't have to necessarily stay there, because God is willing to forgive us for our sins. He wants us to return home again, His doors are always open to receive us

He wants us to admit our faults and disobedience; and he will not be angry with us forever (Jeremiah 3:12-13).

We are more than conquerors. We do not have to live defeated lives. We don't have to live broken or frustrated lives. God created us and gave us all we need to be happy creatures.

Only the Lord can make you whole, the same way that He has made me whole. God can destroy the enemy that is invading your life, and that can be achieved only through his Word and the leading of the Holy Spirit.

He loves you and cares for you.

He is ready to restore your brokenness; He is ready to heal your soul as He healed mine. He is ready to equip you with all you need to defeat the past and the enemy who is constantly invading your life. You have to be willing to trust Him to change and get to a better place.

God never wanted you to be broken or remain broken. He never wanted bad things to happen to you. He says, "For I know the plans I have for you. They are plans for good and not for disaster, to give you a future and a hope" *(*Jeremiah 29:11*)*

Quote to Ponder:

"God saw it good and appropriate to plant his seeds into my heart. He kept me yearning for his Word"

Chapter Notes

Work It Out

Memorize:

Romans 3:23

"For everyone has sinned; we all fall short of God's glorious standard".

Journal:

Prompt:

God has given each of us free will and the ability to choose right and wrong. Do you think that God should prevent all evil and wrongdoings that are happening in our world?

Pray:

Thank you Lord for opening up my eyes to the brokenness of the world. Help me Lord to seek you for my healing and brokenness.

Chapter 3

Self-Awareness: Connecting the Impact of Your Past on Your Life

"When I discover who I am, I'll be free."
— *Ralph Ellison,* **Invisible Man**

"I don't like people; I do not trust them." Have you ever heard that statement before? I have heard it more than I care to count. People often say that casually as if it has no bearing on how they live.

They expect you to take it at face value. I certainly commend them for the courage to even say that aloud, but when pushed as to why they do not like or trust people, they seem to be at a loss for words.

If you spend long enough to know a little bit about them, you will notice that there is no presence of deep relationships in their lives and often they find ways to sabotage themselves when good opportunities come their way. Trust is a foreign territory for them.

My version of that statement has a twist to it. I like everybody, but I do not trust them. As a matter of fact, I never met a person I did not like. Despite so many negative experiences I endured in my life, I still see the glass half full. I am not exaggerating; I am too positive for my own good. That often translates into having my guard down and not holding people accountable for their actions.

In the spirit of self-awareness, a statement like the one mentioned above and behavior of not holding people accountable for their actions do not just happen to us, we create and live them every day because we fail to make the connection between our past and our present behavior. So we keep getting invaded by an unknown enemy with tremendous power over our thoughts and our actions.

Self-awareness is having a clear and thorough understanding of who you are, your strengths, weaknesses, vulnerabilities, your capabilities, and how all these things can work together as you make progress towards life. As New York Times Bestselling author John C. Maxwell states in his book No Limits: Blow the Cap off your Potential,

> Self-awareness is a powerful skill; it enables you to see yourself clearly. It informs your decisions and helps you to weigh opportunities. It allows you to test your limits. It empowers you to understand other people. It makes your partnership with others stronger. It allows you to maximize your weaknesses. It opens the door to a greater capacity.

The question is how can you change something that you are not aware of? That is precisely the point, you have to get curious about yourself, your needs, your desires, and the contributions you want to make in this world. You have to evaluate your motives, self-talk, habits, and any excuses you may have been practicing. Here are a few questions you can ask yourself that can help you develop a clear understanding of who you are.

What Do I Need to Know?

That seems to be a moot point you say, if you knew what you were supposed to do, you would do it, right? You may be partially right. Perhaps, you are that person who does what you know you have to do. But so many of us know what we need to do and still does not do it. If you want to be a conqueror and change your life, you must be willing to do the work.

Let your interests, goals, desires, wants, relationships, and experiences to inform your quest to self-awareness. Spend time with yourself and reflect on your decisions and how they impact they your progress.

What Do I Need to Do?

Developing your self-awareness can be hard. We tend to focus our attention on where we are weak, so the work to get to our desired self seems like Mt. Everest. Since we do not want to be average, we are not going to focus on our weaknesses, we will focus on our strengths.

When we focus on our strengths, we open up our path to greatness. To achieve that greatness, we must put our self-awareness discoveries to action.

Get Clear on the Enemy

To become a conqueror, we must realize that we are at war.

We are at war with an enemy that does not always come to us with weapons drawn, but often subtle, with a smile and the perks of victimhood rendering us unable to confront the facts of our choices in people we allow to influence our lives, the environment we subject ourselves to, the daily decisions we make, the behaviors we keep repeating, and our attitudes toward all these points.

Our fuzzy vision of the enemy enables us to remain in our comfort zones.

We are at war. We are always at war, even when you do not think so. Living life seems to be a constant battle. We are often frustrated because we are unable to pinpoint the enemy.

Who is the opponent that keeps invading our lives with the mistake of the past? Who stands in the way of our relationships with God, our spouses, with our family, and with the community at large? Who works diligently every day to destroy your future?

No one likes to talk about Satan. That just seems like a cop-out. The reality is Satan is the ultimate enemy since the Garden of Eden. He is the source of all sins in this broken world. His mission is to discover every opportunity to kill, steal and destroy (John 10:10).

He does not want anything good for you; he does not want you to flourish. He wants to completely destroy you. So invading you with your past mistakes, traumas, losses, and pain are tools that he often uses to keep you stuck day after day, week after weeks, and year after year. Before you know it, decades have gone by while you think the same thoughts, do the same things and dream the same dreams.

That is why James admonishes us to "so give yourselves to God. Stand against the devil, and he will run away from you" (4:7 ERV). Know this enemy well because he is a tricky one. He is bold too. He is deceitful, often disguising himself as the angel of light.

He even tempted Jesus himself quoting scriptures. Jesus rebuked him by also quoting scripture to the devil. In the same way, we need to understand that we have the power and the authority to defeat Satan. Luke states, "Look, I have given you authority over all the power of the enemy, and you can walk among snakes and scorpions and crush them. Nothing will injure you" (10:19 NLT).

To keep Satan from invading our present and destroying our future, there are certain things that we must understand, believe, and do. Take notes of the following:

1. Jesus defeated the devil on the cross.

The battle is already won. Jesus conquered the devil on the cross. He came to destroy the works of the devil in the lives of his children. Therefore, Satan has no authority over us – to invade our present with the past and to destroy the future that God has intended for us. He can only assume authority over our lives if we are ignorant of who we are in Christ, oblivious of the power and weapons at our disposal, and lack of training necessary to resist him whenever he decides to attack us in his chosen area of our lives.

Only God can relinquish that authority for a certain purpose as in the life of Job. Otherwise, Satan does not stand a chance against us and our God. It is our responsibility to take this victory and the authority given to us to conquer the devil whenever he chooses to attack us and our family.

2. We have spiritual weapons at our disposal.

As a young girl, I loved books. I would save my sporadic allowances to buy them. However, I could not read them, so I would look at the pages from time to time, touching the letters with my fingers.

I did not have parents who understood the different levels of reading at the time, as a result for years, the only thing I did with the few books that I collected was look and touch the pages.

As can be imagined, I remained ignorant concerning what was written in the books and how valuable it may be. In the same way, God has given us spiritual weapons to conquer the devil such as the name of Jesus, the cross of Jesus, the blood of Jesus, and the Word of God. How will they have any value and effect on our lives if we do not use them?

3. Take Responsibility

You are a conqueror! You are a warrior! You are not a helpless victim for the devil to toy around with whenever he wishes. Our self-perception of who we are in Christ is ultimately the catalyst that Satan uses to invade your present and destroy your future.

If we are not confident in our relationship with Christ and have no idea where we stand with God, we are vulnerable. We must see ourselves as a very powerful child of God who has the authority to crush snakes and scorpions, conquer the Goliaths in our lives knowing that we do not walk alone, but with the Host of Heaven's armies.

We do not walk alone and we are never alone, so start acting like the conqueror you are and put that helpless victim to the side.

4. Make a Commitment to Obey God's Word.

This is where we will learn about who we are and who we are supposed to become. This is where we learn about our God and what he has done. This is where we learn about the power, authority, tools, and strategies for everyday battles. This is where we are encouraged by those who have fought before us. This is where we study the enemy, his ultimate goal, and how to conquer him. Making a commitment to spend time learning God's Word is extremely important in ensuring victory over the weak areas of our lives.

5. Stay Out of Your Own Way

"The devil made me do it." "I just can't help it; I can't seem to do anything right." When we use these statements, we voluntarily give our power away and risk our victory, since the devil cannot make you do anything you do not want to do.

We know Satan has a job to do here on earth and that is to keep you as distracted as possible, so that you will not focus on what matters most.

Why would you want to help him?

Yes, we help Satan when we blame him for what he is not responsible for. When we ascribe powers to him that he does not have, we weaken our resolve to respond to events that happens in our lives. We must take inventory on our self-sabotage habits, and work diligently into replacing them with productive ones.

Quote to Ponder:

"Satan has no authority over us –

to invade our present with the past

and to destroy the future that God

has intended for us."

Chapter Notes

Work It Out

Memorize:

James 4:7

…so give yourself to God. Stand against the devil, and he will flee from you".

Journal:

Prompt:

What about your past that is preventing you from becoming a conqueror? What about the past that is holding you back? How is your awareness of this problem a great help in solving it?

Pray:

Lord, help me see clearly all the obstacles that prevent me from becoming all that you have intended for me to become.

Chapter 4

The Invasion

"It is not love that keeps us stuck in the past.
Love fades over time. What introspective hearts
seek is simply unanswered questions
about why terrible things
can happen to very good people.
Closure never comes
from reflection. It only comes from
God's guidance and promptings."

— *Shannon L. Alder*

I was not ready to listen to God's calling. I still thought that I could survive without God and did not need Him in my life. God had abandoned me to the cruelty of the world, and I was not willing to welcome Him back into my life.

Why should I trust someone who had allowed those terrible things happen to me? Moreover, awful things happened not only to me but also to thousands of other innocent people across the world. It was almost as if God was enjoying the misery on the planet and was hoping to inflict even more pain.

I refused to return back to the church for many years. I stayed away from it and I strongly believed I was happy with my life. I felt quite fine and was able to conduct my affairs and daily routines quite well, giving little thought to the Bible. That was until one day when I saw the light and sought to return back into God's arms and into His family.

For the last fourteen years, it has been a wonderful and nurturing journey to learn and experience the awesome love of God. It has not been easy, I can assure you of that, but I discovered that if you open yourself to Him, He will restore you to your rightful place and heal you completely from each and every wound that have been inflicted on you.

Your wounds may be different from mine; however, pain is always pain. Whether you have been physically, sexually or psychologically abused, or if you frequently experience thoughts of suicide, hopelessness and worthlessness, the Lord has a cure for you. That cure is Jesus Christ.

Over the recent past years, I learned how to become a conqueror refusing to let my past invade my present and destroy my future. Learning to love Jesus again opened my eyes to the rest of my life and the many possibilities to create a happy and productive life.

When in September 2009 McKenzie Phillips, a former child star, revealed to Larry King and also to Oprah Winfrey that she had been sexually abused by her father, the rock legend John Phillips, I could not help feeling an agonizing pain growing inside me.

I understood her because I knew her pain. I, too, had been sexually abused by my father and, as a result of it, I had suffered a lot through all the past years.

As I continued following McKenzie's heartbreaking story, I learned how so many people were empowered by her story and, at last, they felt they were not alone. However, the pain seemed more apparent than ever. It was as if they were living the abuse all over again. I ached for them.

I prayed for them. I wished that I could reach and hug them and tell them that they didn't have to do it alone. They were not alone! I started to think about how I could let them know they were not alone! How could I reach them and transmit them what I had learned?

My experiences taught me that many people who have suffered any kind of abuse, whether physical, emotional, psychological, verbal, or sexual have the difficulty of not letting it go. They are apparently hooked to it and they have no idea how their past life affects their present life and eventually their future life.

They do not have the perspective to realize that they are repeating the same mistakes over and over again. Because they cannot see the past for what it is, they cannot learn from it and embrace the future. It is necessary to brake the chains that keep us tied to the past and prevent us from moving on.

People that keep ties to their painful pasts see themselves as victims, those who have voluntarily given away their power to the past, other people, bad habits, and to circumstances.

As a result, they do everything based on a victim's mindset. They are seriously and in some ways completely blind when it comes to realizing how directly linked past behavior and present behavior are.

Defining Invasion

If we do some honest introspection, most of us will have to admit that we have done one or more things that we are not proud of. For instance, you may have…

- ✓ Been rebellious and messed up your life as well as the lives of some other people
- ✓ Cheated on your significant other and having a romantic relationship has never been the same after that
- ✓ Told lies to people who trusted you
- ✓ Stolen things that did not belong to you
- ✓ Instigate conflicts to cause division
- ✓ Injured someone through your bad habits

The list goes on and on. The reality is that if you want to make a list of things you have done wrong in your life, you will never stop writing. It is not so just for you; it is the same for me. It is in our human nature to have negative or harmful thoughts, say inappropriate things or do some things that God would frown upon.

These are natural behaviors, and it is normal to do all these things when you have walked away from the Lord. Human nature leads us to do bad things and things that we are not proud of.

If we simply do what we want to do without having some consideration for the others, if we act just following our own will, we may get to experience a momentary feeling of freedom, a liberating sensation of living fully in that precise moment. But with some reflection, guilt may hit us; and even if we do not know what is causing that guilt, we will still feel it nonetheless.

That unexplainable sense of guilt comes from deep inside; it comes from the inner knowledge that we have moved away from God's intended plan or design.

Anyone can experience this feeling, and it is a signal that indicates to us that we need to address the root cause rather than seeking to address only the external symptoms.

One of these symptoms may be loneliness, and we may try to cure this by constantly seeking out for new people. However, if we do not discriminate in our choices and make friends with the wrong people or in the wrong place, this will not solve the problem.

Maybe we seek to find comfort in unlimited sex or we may start to experiment with drugs or alcohol. All these things may bring us great pleasure and enjoyment for a moment. We may feel fulfilled, living the present moment in plenitude and enjoying all that is available to satisfy our senses.

Still, the pleasure will subside as we become accustomed to the new sensations. We may get to feel that nothing suffices so we will want to go for more and newer sensations. We may seek out new and more extreme experiences until the quest becomes more part of the pleasure than the experience itself.

God tells us that many of these things that bring us pleasure are sins and therefore, should not be done. We must understand that God is not simply trying to withhold all the good stuff for Himself or to deprive us of pleasure merely for malicious purposes. God knows that sinning can become addictive.

To be in love without the tears of regret or to get high with a heartache of stone can be rewarding and bring great freedom to an individual. But that will be just for a little while. However, God is wise and He knows that the world must be balanced and, receiving great pleasure will also bring great pain.

The extreme ends of the spectrum are inexplicably linked and with great rewards and great risks. With pleasure comes pain, it's easy as that. This is why we must abstain ourselves from such practices.

Even if the activities tempting us appear harmless or pleasurable to us, we should be aware of the fact that our actions and decisions always carry a consequence and will probably result in unforeseen results.

Perhaps you were not the cause of someone's pain but someone inflicted pain on you. Some of you may have been subject to physical, sexual, or emotional abuse during the most innocent years of your lives.

The ones who were supposed to love and care for you were twisted enough to take advantage of you, the ones who should have protected you were, in fact, the ones that did harm you or, it may have been a total stranger who came from nowhere and turned your life upside down.

Some of us may have been broken by natural disasters such as: hurricanes, earthquakes, tornadoes, or mudslides that seemed to have destroyed everything in their paths. Or maybe it was a terrorist attack such as the (9/11) what left you stricken with grief and loss.

It could have been a disease that seemed to have popped up out of nowhere what actually broke you. Or possibly you had the perfect family and then they were taken from you as a result of a tragic accident.

Do not think I am heartless when I make such a cruel list? I am not rubbing it in, I am just being realistic and saying things as they are. I don't want to hurt you any further, but I want to open your eyes to the information that the enemy uses to invade our lives.

I want you to become aware. Webster's 2nd Riverside Dictionary defined the word invade as follows:

1. To go into by force so as to conquer or pillage.
2. To enter and overrun harmfully.
3. To encroach upon: violate."

Satan would like nothing more for you than seeing you hurt and broken. So, he goes around playing tricky mind games with you. His goal is to keep you confused, not knowing the difference between good or bad, guilt or innocence, bondage or freedom. Satan wants you to remain ignorant about the magnificence of your potential.

Satan is a master at inserting himself into everything, ranging from the most ordinary routine activity to the holiest of the texts. Satan manages to corrupt individuals in such a way that even the most religious person can fall under his malicious spell. Consider the amount of evil done in the name of the Lord. Think of the course of history and the countless numbers of lost lives and the vast volumes of blood that have been shed in the name of God. Religion has been perverted and bent to serve a purpose for which it is not intended.

Satan can slip into the unguarded life of anyone within the blink of an eye and, unless you are ever diligent, you can be put to work to serve him without you ever realizing it. Every time he uses your past against you, his intention is to harm and to violate you. Satan will try to invade you in any of the following ways:

1. Blaming Ourselves

People like to figure things out. They want to be able to say that "a" equals "b". They want to have a clear and logical explanation about why certain things happen to them.

For example, a woman who has been victim of rape maybe invaded by negative thoughts that keep telling her that if she had not dressed in a certain way, she would not have been raped. It was not her fault, but she still feels guilty for the harm that was inflicted to her, she feels like she deserved it.

That is definitely wrong. However, that is what the enemy does. He wants this woman to believe that she asked to be raped, she deserved it and she should stay right where she is—under his malevolent control.

Satan is the master of deceit. He is crafty when it comes to using our own downfalls and insecurities against us. He knows how hurt and vulnerable we are. He knows how battered we are. He knows we don't look at ourselves favorably, so he attacks and makes us feel guilty. His hope is to help you dig a deep hole, deeper than the one that is trapping you today. When we are immersed in the hole; we do not see the world for what it is.

We view it from the submerged perspective we have. We are given false illusions and are prevented from viewing things as they really are. We may believe that we are right, and we will ignore all evidence showing the contrary. More than often we blindly ignore what is right beneath our noses and we view and interpret things through the prism of our own experiences and senses.

We cannot evaluate things objectively. We may not be brave enough to disregard this information and act in a counter intuitive way. It seems to us that those who criticize us are wrong and are trying to lead us astray. What happens is that our own judgment has become perverted and therefore, we continue living within the cycle of self-destruction.

We misinterpret the visual and sensual feedback received from the world around us and we continue wandering, lost, without guidance, obeying only our basic instincts or impulses and aiming to obtain pleasure from short-term activities. It is quite possible to live one's entire life in this way and, moreover, to do so without feeling any remorse or angst.

Only occasionally will one awaken and have some brief moments of clarity, and then realize that this is not the life that God wishes us to have. God created us to be happy, he is our heavenly Father and, as any loving father, He wants us to be free, good and happy individuals.

2. Blaming Others

Satan invades us with our past by feeding us with negative messages that force us to blame others for our current condition. For instance, your parents may have hurt you because they failed to be home as much as you needed it. Often, they worked all day long. Their intentions were not to hurt you— their intentions were to provide for you, but unintentionally they failed and hurt us somehow.

Satan leads us to think they are guilty and responsible for our hurt feelings. More often than not, we can understand this scenario. But what hurts the most is when someone intentionally harms us.

Like the child who cried after having had been abused only to be ridiculed and dismissed.

Satan uses these opportunities to feed us with negative messages that trigger our pain. He wants us to believe that the past equals the present and the future. However, that is absolutely false. We could not control what happened to us in the past, but we can control how we respond to it now.

We have the necessary inner tools to decide how to deal with what happened to us and to put a final stop to the damage. Time is treated in a non-linear manner and all events seem to be occurring simultaneously. Both the action and the consequence are so deeply linked that it is impossible to talk about one without talking about the other.

Attempting to impose reason upon this situation is akin to pouring water on chip pan fire. The reaction will be disastrous. As the current situation is not one created out of reason, but emerging from the depths of human nature, an alternative solution is necessary. Refuge can be found in the plans the Lord has for each and all of us; but so many people are unable to comprehend it because they do not look to the light in the right way.

3. Blaming God

When we lose a beloved one due to death or to a fatal disease, we tend to blame God for it. How could He allow it? After all, God is in control. Isn't He? Satan wants you to doubt that God is on your side because he knows that God is the only one who can heal and restore your brokenness.

So, he constantly invades you with negative thoughts about how God does not care for you at all. Since his goal is to keep you broken, defeated, ineffective and unproductive, he wants you to distrust God. This happens because he knows you cannot have a productive relationship with someone whom you don't trust.

This system works well for both parties involved and allows the fallen person to keep walking without blame and shame. They feel secure in the knowledge that nothing they have done has to do with their present and that their problems have not actually manifested themselves through any action they have taken.

The responsibility and cause of the situation can be shifted onto a non-existent God who will take the blame and yet be simultaneously invisible. This highly illogical frame of mind is engendered by Satan, the great divider who weaves a web of lies to blind us from the true nature of the world merely to keep us trapped in the mist and darkness. However, so great are His powers that we will not even be aware that this has happened.

Instead, we will most likely choose to ignore the horrors around us and, like a war in a foreign country, we will walk on untouched. Looking ourselves in the mirror, we do not see our true image and instead we project a vision that is reflected back to us in a corrupt manner.

Quote to Ponder:

"Satan can slip into the unguarded life of anyone within the blink of an eye and, unless you are ever diligent, you can be put to work to serve him without you ever realizing it."

Chapter Notes

<u>Work It Out</u>

Memorize:

John 10:10

The thief comes only in order to steal and kill and destroy. I came that they may have and enjoy life, and have it in abundance [to the full, till it overflows]

Journal:

Prompt:

In what way do you see the past repeating itself in your everyday life? How do you see yourself playing the blaming game? What specific actions will you take today to demonstrate to yourself that you are now taking responsibility for yourself?

Pray:

Lord, help me see the experiences of my past with a growth mindset. Help me to learn the important lessons, so I will not repeat the same situations blocking me from enjoying the present.

Chapter 5

The Battles We Fight

"While winners were fully engaged
with writing some great chapters in their lives,
failures were busy trying to edit their past
negative experiences."
— *Edmond Mbiaka*

How do you know when you are being invaded by your past? How do you become conscious of that invasion from the past? That is a very good question. People who have a sad past, whether it is abuse, loss, rejection, or any sort of difficulty, are frequently unaware of the effects that such past produce on their present lives.

The past is such a big part of their daily lives that they cannot recognize or they cannot make the connection between the past on their current behaviors. They love their brokenness because it helps them to remain in the "victim" category. They enjoy perks such as attention and pity.

Therefore, if this is your case too, it is imperative that you become aware of the typical problems, attitude, and behaviors of a victim in order to be able to plan and begin your inner change.

Neediness Keeps You from Creating Meaningful Relationships

As the adage goes, if we keep doing what we always do, we will get what we've always gotten. People whose pasts are holding them back, keep doing the same thing over and over again despite of the fact that it is not productive or beneficial. They constantly surround themselves with people who support their negative behaviors and cater to all their needs.

Valerie is a clear example of that, she knows too well how to manipulate her family to get what she wants. All she has to do is whine her way through it. She loves telling the same old stories about terrible things that happened to her long time ago. Sure enough, she always gets what she wants. It is easy for Valerie to act in such a manner.

However, it is harder for her to face the truth and make better choices to move her out of this victimized way of living. To do that, she should surround herself with people who have the guts to tell her the truth. Although the people who have allowed her to get to do what she wants may be good intentioned, they are not helping her to live in the proper way to facilitate her to develop her full potential.

It is a recurrent fact that happens to most of us: we are being invaded by our pasts when we take more than we give.

When Comfort Is Not
All It Cracked to Be

If we observe ourselves with sincerity, we will all acknowledge that we have comfort zones. It is in our human nature to stay in our comfort zones rather than to explore the unknown. At times, it does not matter if our comfort zones are unproductive or demeaning. It is easier to remain within what is familiar for us because we know how to respond to it, we are accustomed to dealing with it

Take John for example, his parents always talked and treated him in such a way that they led him to think that he would never be able to achieve much in life. He strongly convinced himself of that, because if his parents said so, it had to be true. He wouldn't question it.

Consequently, he spent most of his adult life poisoning his body with drugs and alcohol. After all, it didn't matter, it would not make a difference. Although John was deeply hurt, he found it too hard to change. It was easier for him to remain in this harming cycle, because it was familiar to him—he knew what to expect.

When we find ourselves suffering in a familiar place where we are unproductive, disrespected, and unloved, yet we don't do anything to move forward and continue to stay there—we are indeed being invaded by our pasts.

Revenge Often Leads to More Trouble

When I started my doctorate program, I took a job at the local juvenile assessment center where I worked with teens and young adults whose mission in life seemed to be to destroy themselves considering the way they were living. They were doing drugs, skipping school, running away from home, fighting, and getting in trouble with the law.

They were very bright children but they did not care about their futures. Those who cared about them felt like they were living in hell, suffering from seeing their loved loves destroying their lives and their families again and again, and they kept attempting to rescue those rebel kids from themselves.

After evaluating them and their behaviors, I learned they were somehow determined to destroy themselves, because that was their way of taking revenge on their families. They had been lied to, cursed at, disappointed, abused, hurt, ignored and violated by their families.

And quite simply, their behaviors and attitudes were direct and obvious messages telling that they are were now in control of themselves. Those young boys and girls mistakenly thought that they had the power to do as they wish.

If you are now living in that situation—you are being invaded by your past.

Interdependence not Dependence

People who grew up in families where they were nurtured, loved and encouraged to become healthy adults; do not crave for inappropriate attention and affection. We can say that they are balanced individuals. They learned to give as well as to receive.

There are some who are not as fortunate though. Their family lives lacks genuine affection, care, and a sense of approval. They do not feel responsible for their own happiness. They find it easier to put the burdens and responsibility for their happiness on their loved ones.

When you find yourself too dependent on your parents, friends, spouses, and others for your well-being, growth, and happiness—you are being invaded by your past.

Excuses Keep You Stuck

No one gets anywhere with excuses. Yet many people find excuses as plausible routes through their lives. Do you know why people love making excuses for their pathetic and unproductive lives? Simply because it is easier to blame on others than to recognize our own responsibility when things don't turn out as we expected.

It takes courage and determination to keep taking risks until you get it right. It takes courage to take responsibility for every action whether it is good or bad. We have to be brave and humble to admit that we are the ones in charge of ourselves, that we are responsible of our decisions, actions and their consequences. That is not easy. That is hard work.

Excuses create a constant revolving door when you refuse to learn from your past. You keep doing the same thing over and over again. Making excuses will lead you to bigger problems.

You are being invaded by your past when your life is wrapped around excuses.

Challenges Are Meant to Strengthen You

It is not unusual to see that people who are being invaded by their pasts, tend to avoid challenges at all costs. They do not want to jeopardize the familiar place. They feel safe in this place they know well, no matter how destructive it may actually be.

Sam is a good example of such attitude. After college, he was given several opportunities to move to other states to start a great career. He was reluctant to accept those offers. Two of the companies increased his starting salary to entice him.

There was still no positive response from him. Even though the job offers were promising, Sam rejected them, he didn't have the courage to accept the challenge of moving forward to the unknown, even when the conditions seemed favorable and promising.

So, instead of moving on for a better future, for his own personal growth, he decided to stay with the same family members who were constantly degrading him. He unconsciously created an excuse for that, the excuse he found was to think that now it was his duty to take care of them.

"They would not have known what to do without me," he said. The sad reality is that Sam was unwilling to try a new environment because it was scary for him.

When you avoid challenges on a regular basis because you are afraid of losing your safety net—you are being invaded.

Self-Centeredness Makes You a god

We all have friends or family members that at one moment or another, try to be the center of everything. They keep doing things to get attention. They are very creative when it comes to making every conversation go around them and their needs.

They seem to have a natural skill to become the center of attention. It looks like they were the belly button of the world. They are in perpetual need of the care and attention that they are unable to give to the others.

When you use your past to manipulate people to get what you want you are being invaded.

Refusing to Change Keeps You in the Past

Change is hard, and at times it can be downright scary. Change is not for cowards because change is defying. It is for people who know that they deserve something better and are willing to take their chances and bet on them. But when you refuse to change, you are telling the world that you don't deserve good things in life. You may be stuck in your painful and ugly circumstances because that's what's comfortable and safe.

That is what you are used to, that is what you know and you don't have the courage to accept the challenge of making a change. But unless you change, your circumstances will remain, and you will keep living similar situations.

Don't blame it on the circumstances, you are not a victim; the responsibility is yours. You are the one that can make those painful circumstances turn into positive ones, but the change has to start with you and in you.

It takes courage to go against what seems natural or normal to us since it is what we know. It takes perseverance to enter and stay within the path of change. You must be patient with yourself knowing things will get better with small and consistent actions.

When you find yourself in destructive circumstances and yet change seems not to be an option for you to take—you are indeed being invaded by your past.

Quote to Ponder:

"People whose pasts are holding them back, keep doing the same thing over and over again despite of the fact that it is not productive or beneficial."

Chapter Notes

_____

_____

_____

_____

_____

_____

_____

_____

_____

_____

_____

_____

_____

_____

_____

_____

_____

_____

_____

_____

_____

_____

_____

_____

_____

Work It Out

Memorize:

Joshua 24:15

"Choose you this day whom you will serve, but as for me and my house, we will serve the Lord".

Journal:

Prompt:

Dwelling in the past for no good reason is a choice. Working hard at changing the experiences of the past is a choice. How will you know when you have made the decision to learn from the past instead of having it control you?

Pray: "Lord, help me to focus on the lessons to be learned from the past instead of trying to change it".

Chapter 6

Victim or Conqueror

"You are not a victim.

No matter what you have been through,

you're still here.

You may have been challenged, hurt, betrayed,

beaten, and discouraged, but nothing has defeated

you.

You are still here!

You have been delayed but not denied.

You are not a victim; you are a victor.

You have a history of victory."

— *Steve Maraboli,*

Unapologetically You: Reflections on Life

and the Human Experience

At times, we forget that we live in a broken
world, where we exercise the free will that God has
given us, whether that is for good or for bad. So, we

hurt each other and we are often the subject of pain and suffering.

The problem arises when we get stuck in a state of victimhood as if living in the past is better and safer than living in the present. We continually destroy the potential of our future because we continually decide not to take positive action today. If we want to change our lives and stop being a slave to our past, we must decide either to be a victim or a conqueror.

What is the difference between the two?

I recently read an article by Mateo Sol that provided 23 signs of the victim mentality. Before we go on to the signs, he provided a definition which helps to clarify this mindset. He states,

> "Victim mentality is a psychological term that refers to a type of dysfunctional mindset which seeks to feel persecuted in order to gain attention or avoid self-responsibility. People who

struggle with the victim mentality are convinced that life is not only beyond their control, but is out to deliberately hurt them."

What struck me about this definition is that the victim mentality "seeks to feel persecuted" to enjoy the rewards that comes with this mindset. Some of these rewards may include but are not limited to not taking responsibility, being the center of attention, and getting our way.

So, we choose to stay in a torturous state so we can manipulate people and therefore avoid the hard work that is necessary to have a good and productive life.

To some, that may be a source of power, knowing that we can avoid taking responsibility for what we say, what we do, and how we behave. Others, get a kick out of seeing how their manipulations affect the people closest to them.

The other thing that struck me about this definition is the point that people with a victim mentality are "convinced that life is deliberately out to hurt them." As a result of this mindset, fear and anger abound and there is always enough blame to go around.

As Byron Katie, the author of Loving What Is: Four Questions That Can Change Your Life states,

> As long as you think that the cause of your problem is "out there"—as long as you think that anyone or anything is responsible for your suffering—the situation is hopeless. It means that you are forever in the role of victim that you're suffering in paradise.

So, the whole notion of the comfort zone comes to play. It is hard to make changes in our comfort zones.

Here are Sol's 23 signs of the victim mentality:

- ✓ You're constantly blaming other people or situations for feeling miserable
- ✓ You possess a "life is against me" philosophy
- ✓ You're cynical or pessimistic
- ✓ You see your problems as catastrophes and blow them out of proportion
- ✓ You think others are purposely trying to hurt you
- ✓ You believe you're the only one being targeted for mistreatment
- ✓ You keep reliving past painful memories that made you feel like a victim
- ✓ Even when things go right, you find something to complain about
- ✓ You refuse to consider other perspectives when talking about your problems
- ✓ You feel powerless and unable to cope effectively with a problem or life in general
- ✓ You feel attacked when you're given constructive criticism
- ✓ You believe you're not responsible for what happens in your life (others are)

- ✓ You believe that everyone is "better off" than you
- ✓ You seem to enjoy feeling sorry for yourself
- ✓ You attract people like you (who complain, blame, and feel victimized by life)
- ✓ You believe that the world is a scary, mostly bad, place
- ✓ You enjoy sharing your tragic stories with other people
- ✓ You have a habit of blaming, attacking, and accusing those you love for how you feel
- ✓ You feel powerless to change your circumstances
- ✓ You expect to gain sympathy from others, and when you don't get it, you feel upset
- ✓ You refuse to analyze yourself or improve your life
- ✓ You tend to "one-up" people when it comes to sharing traumatic experiences
- ✓ You're constantly putting yourself down

Take the time to read the 23 signs of the victim mindset again. Where do you see yourself on the list? Write down a few signs you intend to explored to activate your conquering mindset. List them below.

1_____

2._____

3._____

As the opening quote by Steve Maraboli indicated, despite all that has happened to you, perhaps you were betrayed, abused, abandoned, teased, ridiculed, beaten, ignored, or harassed, you are not defeated. You can embrace the changes required for a better future.

Become a Conqueror

In her book, Bad Childhood Good Life, Dr. Laura Schlessinger, a seven-time New York Times Bestselling author provides some perspective on the conqueror mentality and she states,

The obvious question is, "What makes some people hold onto being a victim and others choose to improve their lives?" The answer is control. When you are a perpetual victim, the past is in control of your present. When you are a conqueror, the present is controlled by your choices, in spite of the pain and the pull of your past.

Why aren't we all conquerors?

Being a conqueror requires grit. It requires that we challenge our victimhood for everything that it stands for (see the list above) and step by step break each wall that stands in our way of improving our lives. Here are a few things to start today to become the conqueror that you were always meant to be:

1. Resist the allure of victimhood, embrace who God says you are.

2. Surround yourself with people who are committed to helping you become a conqueror and remove yourself from those who encourage your helpless state of mind.

3. Change your routine, it can facilitate change for the better or for the worst.

4. Choose forgiveness over revenge.

5. Give up the excuses.

Quote to Ponder:

"Conquerors understand that they have one incredible power and that is the power to choose to make good decisions despite the painful pull of the past."

Chapter Notes

_____

_____

_____

_____

_____

_____

_____

_____

_____

_____

_____

_____

_____

_____

_____

_____

_____

_____

_____

_____

_____

Work It Out

Memorize:

Psalm 139:14

"...I am fearfully and wonderfully made".

Journal:

Prompt:

When did you decide to be a conqueror? How has your behavior and attitude toward yourself and others changed?

Pray: Thank you Lord for helping me to know and understand that I am more than a conqueror. I have won over my battles, because you made it possible.

Chapter 7

Courage Gets You into the Arena

"It takes courage to grow up and become who you really are."

— E.E. Cummings

Courage is a word that always seems too big to handle and to claim as my own. The definition alone as provided by Meriam-Webster dictionary is a bit intimidating.

> The mental or moral strength to venture, persevere, and withstand danger, fear, or difficulty.

Courage is a word that demands you to take initiative and to maintain stickability. Courage requires strength and I did not think I possessed that. It is a word that is associated with people who embodies fearlessness and bravery. People like Michelle and Barack Obama, Oprah Winfrey, Nelson Mandela, Toni Morrison, Martin Luther King, and the like of Elie Wiesel.

Nobel Prize winners, presidents, chief executive officers, award-winning journalists, and famous activists. People who are not afraid to confront injustice anywhere and who are steadfast in their beliefs no matter what the price they would have to pay.

In my journey of becoming a conqueror and hearing from people who have struggled with their pasts, I have learned that courage is much broader than that. For some of us even waking up in the morning requires courage to keep the past from invading our present and destroying our future.

Daily moments require us to take risks and confront scary, dubious, repetitive, difficult, overwhelming, and challenging situations. The courage to make these daily choices and decisions moment by moment help us to slowly remove layers of doubt, fear, and self-hatred, revealing little by little opportunities to become the real you.

Now, I see courage everywhere. The decision to stand up to a controlling parent. Asking for a raise because you know your worth. Giving up excuses and taking action when everyone expects you to fall. Giving up a toxic friend. Making a new friend. Saying "No." Following your dreams. Asking for help. Taking the first step.

As stated in the last chapter, being a victim can be very addictive, so refraining oneself from manipulating people to get your toxic ways can be a very hard thing to do. Giving up the bad habits that led to this manipulation is a courageous act.

In her book Daring Greatly: How the Courage to Be Vulnerable Transforms the Way We Live, Love, Parent, and Lead, Brene Brown reminds us that there is strength in sharing our vulnerabilities and until we are able to do so, the transformation will be difficult. Sharing our vulnerabilities comes with great risks because we are coming from being invisible to being visible and that requires courage.

As you become a conqueror and growing your courage, here are a few tips to help you stay grounded in your pursuit of creating the life you intend to live.

1. You Have What It Takes

You were born courageous. You have what it takes inside of you. It will become more apparent as you conquer one difficult situation at a time. The problem with some of us is that the practice of courage has been ridiculed, frowned-upon, or beaten out of us over the course of our lives. Therefore, it is dormant until it gets activated again.

Being a woman of faith has equipped me with the knowledge that the God of the universe is on my side and he will use good and bad experiences for my good, so I am encouraged to step out of my comfort zone and do things thought to be out of my reach perhaps a few months ago. Seek to grow your courage like anything else: one decision at a time.

2. You Will Be Criticized

You are now in the arena for all to see. You are visible both to people who stand ready to help you and those who vehemently disagree with how you are approaching things. That's okay, you must understand that it comes with the territory. Don't be surprised.

I remember when mustered all the courage I had to finally break my silence about being sexually abused. A number of people tried to shut me up because they wanted to protect the criminal instead of me. I tasted freedom when I decided that they would not win.

3. Fail Forward

You are new at this, hence, you are developing your courage to becoming a conqueror. You will make mistakes. Do not let that deter you. Quickly learn from the experience and apply your learning to the next problem you seek to solve.

Will there be "haters" in your face pointing fingers and reminding you that you will not succeed. Absolutely! By now, you have already expected them, so you will not be denied. Simply, take your next step until the battle is won. You will become stronger as a result.

Quote to Ponder:

"There is strength in sharing your vulnerabilities and until we are able to do so, your transformation will be difficult."

<u>Chapter Notes</u>

Work It Out

Memorize:

Deuteronomy 31:6

"Be strong and of good courage."

Journal:

Prompt:

How has it taken courage for you to grow and become who you are?

Pray:

Lord, thank you for keeping me strong to stand against the lure of the past and the courage to live fully in the present.

Chapter 8

Choose Faith over Fear

"None of us knows what might happen even the next minute, yet still we go forward. Because we trust. Because we have Faith."

— *Paulo Coelho,* **Brida**

As you move forward on your journey to become a conqueror, as you work on keeping the past from invading your present and destroying your future, confronting your fears will be one of the most important things you will have to do. It is a natural process; you are embarking on a new venture, a great and overwhelming one like taking responsibility for your life.

You may not see clearly where you are going or feel uncertain about the next step that you need to take. But, the best thing you can do is move forward any way, embracing faith, trusting that on the other side of your decision to move forward is exactly what you need to succeed. Do not let fear bully you out of the choice to take charge of your life.

Giving in to fear can rob you of all that you can become. For as long as I can remember in my late teens and the majority of my twenties, my greatest fear was for my abuse to become known. I did not want to be responsible for messing up my father's reputation and my perfect daughter status. Most people adored him and would never believe that he would do such a thing.

I convinced myself for almost two decades that protecting him was the best thing to do, so I worked hard at creating what looked on the outside to be the best father-daughter relationship you have ever seen. I did such a wonderful job that my cousins and friends wished that they had a father like him. In the meantime, I was dying behind closed doors in the form of depression, timidity, and suicidal ideations.

When I decided to break my silence, it was a last resort, I feared that keeping this secret would be the death of me. My father kept on interfering in my now severely dysfunctional adult life and marriage. I knew deep in my heart I did not want to serve another prison sentence, which was exactly what it felt like.

Family members could not believe how this hard-working, intelligent, and educated young woman such as myself would allow such thing to ever happen. They said that I was lying. Some assert that if it did happen, I loved it because I stayed too long. Nevertheless, with my decision to no longer keep secrets, I opened the door just a little bit for freedom to start sipping in and my resolve to step out on faith and let go of fear got stronger.

Fear can rob you of your very life. Do not miss twenty years of your life because you are afraid of doing something. Conquerors do not act like fear does not exist, we do not run and hide when we are experiencing fear. We do what Deuteronomy admonishes us to do and that is to be strong and courageous in learning the basis for that fear in order to face and conquer it.

This means we have to be accountable for our behavior and action by tackling areas in our lives that need developing or work out difficulties preventing us from going back to school, getting that job, having your own place, setting boundaries, and speaking up for yourself.

We may have experienced different obstacles that may vary our journey, but we all face the damage done head on to move forward despite of fear.

I know that I have shared with you a few loaded examples of how fear has impacted my life. You may not think that your experiences were that severe, I beg you not to discount it. People are afraid of countless things such as driving at night, flying, and speaking in public is preferable to death.

No matter what the fear, it is still debilitating for the person who has it. However, the fears that most of us carry around with us are self-created.

We are most likely to think negatively about the outcomes of our pursuits than we are to think positively about them. They are completely unfounded.

We tend to exaggerate how difficult the path set before us and completely underestimate our abilities to confront and to conquer them.

That is why psychologist utilizes this acronym to describe fear.

- ✓ Fantasized
- ✓ Experiences
- ✓ Appearing
- ✓ Real

Since fear is fantasized and self-created, we can easily shorten its life cycle by choosing faith instead.

It helps us to see our situations and difficulties through God's perspective.

Conquerors choose faith over fear because faith makes our problems appear smaller, renders us expectant of a solution, and gives us the power to keep persevering in the face of insurmountable obstacles. Hebrews 11:1 states,

> What is faith? It is the confident assurance that what

we hope for is going to happen and to be certain of things we do not see.

In his book, The Success Principle: How to Get from Where You Are to Where You Want to Be, bestselling author Jack Canfield shares an exercise that can be helpful in illustrating how we create our own fears.

The format goes as follows:

I want _____, and I scare myself by imagining _____.

Here are a few examples of how I used this exercise.

Created Fears	**Imagined Negative Outcomes**
✓ Speaking in public	➢ I want to speak in public and I scare myself by imagining that I

	will freeze in-front of the audience.
✓ Leaving my job to pursue my dream	➤ I want to leave my job to pursue my dream of writing and speaking and I scare myself by imagining that my family will suffer.
✓ Hiring a sitter	➤ I want to hire a sitter and I scare myself by imagining that my kids will be compromised.
✓ Hiring a coach	➤ I want to hire a coach and I scare myself by imagining that it will be a financial burden.

To continue with this exercise, to get rid of your fears, simply replace your negative imagination with a positive one. Below is an example utilizing the scenarios above.

1. I want to speak in public and I empower myself by imagining my speech changing lives.
2. I want to leave my job and I empower myself by imagining starting a profitable business.
3. I want to hire a sitter and I empower myself by imagining spending quality time with my husband.
4. I want to hire a coach and I empower myself by imagining doubling my income.

This exercise should help you put your fears into perspective. Even Mark Twain realized that his fears were self-imposed when he states, "I have lived a long life and had many troubles, most of which never happened."

You have not come this far in your life without successfully facing some fears, so remember the times when you conquered fear and let that be your blueprint moving forward.

Becoming a conqueror requires you to take a leap of faith to keep the past from invading your present and destroying your future. Go for what you want, no one will give it to you, you have to take it. Let's take your life back.

Quote to Ponder:

"The best thing you can do is move forward, embracing faith, and trusting that on the other side of your decision to move forward is exactly what you need to succeed."

Chapter Notes

Work It Out

Memorize:

2 Timothy 1:7

"For God did not give us a spirit fear, but of power and of love and of a sound mind".

Journal:

Prompt:

What are your fears? How have you replaced them with faith?

Pray: "Lord, help me to exercise my sound mind Amen".

Chapter 9

You Are the Focus of God's Love

Long before He laid down the Earth's
foundations,
He had us in mind, had settled on us as the
focus of His love.

Ephesians 1:4

When you have been abused, misused, wounded, traumatized, disfigured on the outside as well as in the inside, it is hard to believe that you can matter to anyone, especially to God. The truth is that you matter to God, and a lot!

You are not an accident. You are a part of God's beautiful plan. He designed you to be exactly the way you are. He planned every minute of your life, every single detail about you, from the hair on your head to the nails on your toes.

The Bible says: "You watched me as I was being formed in utter seclusion, as I was woven together in the dark of the womb" (Psalm 139:15).

God knew everything about you, including every minimal detail about your life, even before you took your first breath. "You saw me before I was born. Every day of my life was recorded in your book. Every moment was laid out before a single day had passed" (Psalm 139:16). To show how much He cared for you, God created the Earth to be your home before you were born.

God knew exactly where on this Earth would be the best place for you to live. He created that perfect environment for you and everything you could ever need to live a satisfactory life. He knew what would be the best for you. For me, it was the tropical climate of the Caribbean.

Nothing happened randomly, He even chose your parents for you. Your parents may have been the source of your pain, but God knew they had everything He needed to make you the unique person that you are. He knew what you would like and dislike. He knew the line of work you would enjoy.

He had predestined you to be the focus of His love. You are an expression of God's love. He says: "I have cared for you since you were born. Yes, I carried you before you were born. I will be your God throughout your lifetime—until your hair is white with age. I made you, and I will care for you. I will carry you along and save you" (Isaiah 46:3-4).

God did not only create us and everything we would need to survive on Earth, He also promised to be there for us throughout the long haul. His work didn't finish when He created us, He has been and will always be walking by our side, even when some of us do not realize it.

When you are broken into pieces by the troubles of this world, when the odds seem to overwhelm you, God knows exactly how to put you together again. Because He knows how you are formed. When you are in distress and you cry out to Him, He knows exactly what to do to take you out from your troubles and sooth your pain.

Maybe you had a troubled past and it is still tormenting you today? God is love, He loves you unconditionally and He is ready to listen to you. Tell Him what is tormenting you and give Him the chance to heal you. Ask Him for help and relief, ask Him from the depth of your heart and you will receive.

Maybe until this point you thought that your life had no meaning or purpose—that no one cared or loved you. I have good news for you; it's time to change your mind. Your life has a tremendous meaning and a purpose, but if you remain apart from God, you will remain lost.

If you want to understand yourself, you have to immerse yourself in God's love. Get to know Him and what He has done for you. Only then you will understand who you are.

God loves you so much that He gave you free will. He does not demand that you worship Him, He gives you choice and freedom. Regrettably, we often choose to reject Him. He did not leave us to destroy ourselves, He sent His son Jesus to rescue us.

John 3:16 put it this way: "For God so loved the world that He gave His only Son, so that everyone who believes in Him will not perish but have eternal life." God gave His most precious treasure, His son so that He could have the possibility to have a relationship with you.

Isn't that awesome? Can there be a bigger demonstration of love than giving His own son for your salvation?

God did all of this and yet asked He for nothing in return. We have free will and we can choose to turn away from Him and reject the teachings He has given us. This unconditional love is truly remarkable. Where else can such love be found? Maybe in the bond between mother and child? But even children can anger their mothers.

However, God does not give His back to any of His beloved creations: you, me, all of us. He waits for His children (us) to recognize the errors we make and waits for us to voluntarily return back to Him and His love, with no strings attached and no repercussions.

This is why your adversaries and those who wish your harm will strive to keep you away from God. They realize that once you return back into the arms of God, you will see what was hidden from you. Once you realize the extent of God's love and welcome Him back into life, you will surely wonder why you ever stayed away and how you were able to do so for so long.

God will patiently wait for you to return to Him. He created you, you are part of His plan. God has a purpose for you and, if like me, you stayed away or shut him out of your life for a long time, this will only become evident once you give yourself fully Him.

To trust in God and relinquish control to Him may seem like a frightening prospect. Acknowledge these fears but try to understand where they may be stemming from. Why would anyone want to keep you from unconditional love?

When the enemy seeks to use your past to harm you by telling you that because of what you have done or what was done to you, God could not love you—you can tell that person that he/she is an absolute liar. His goal is to push you further away from God.

You can tell that person that God paid a price for your redemption. This scripture is found in 1 Peter 18-20,

> For you know that God paid a ransom to save you from the empty life you inherited from your ancestors. And the ransom He paid was not mere gold or silver. He paid for you with the precious blood of Christ, the sinless, long before the world began, but now in these final days, he was sent to the earth for all to see. And he did this for you.

You are special to God. You are beautiful in His eyes and, according to Genesis 1:27, you were made accordingly to His image. He has placed a wealth of beauty, resoluteness, dignity, resources, and greatness inside of you. Let's take this truth to our hearts and believe it, and God will show you the plan He has for you.

From this day on, decide to see yourself through God's eyes of love. Accept yourself and determine to be all what God intended you to be. Allow yourself to be the wonderful and happy person God created you to be, let His love help you achieve your full potential and happiness.

Don't be afraid, don't be shy to reject people's opinions about you. If it is not in line with the Word of God, then it is a lie. Do not believe it and do not be afraid to confront them.

Quote to Ponder:

"You are special to God. You are
beautiful in His eyes; you were
made according to His image.
He has placed a wealth of beauty,
resoluteness, dignity, resources,
and greatness inside of you."

<u>Chapter Notes</u>

Work It Out

Memorize:

Isaiah 46:3-4

"I have cared for you since you were born. Yes, I carried you before you were born. I will be your God throughout your lifetime—until your hair is white with age. I made you, and I will care for you. I will carry you along and save you".

Journal:

Prompt:

Like I have done many times in my life, have you ever doubted that God cares for you? How has your perspective of God changed over the course of this book?

Pray: Lord, thank you for showing me who you really are and how much you care for me. Amen.

Chapter 10

The Only Savior

"I, even I, am the LORD, and there is no savior besides Me.

Isaiah 43:11

My grandfather was everything to me during my younger years. We were inseparable. It was said that my mother was his favorite, so in my mother's absence he protected me with everything he had and however he could. No one could touch me without feeling his wrath.

When I was taken away from him, without even a single goodbye, to live with my mother, I was heartbroken. Then, a few short years later, I was sent away again. This time to live with my father, and that happened without anyone giving me any explanation. My heart was broken again, for I became quite close to my baby brother. I enjoyed playing with him, picking him up from school, and protecting him.

I was eleven years old when I met my father. Even though everything was different to what I had known and seen before, he and his wife seemed to be caring. Less than six months after my arrival, they separated. It was not long after that, that the molestation and abuse began. I was afraid and didn't have a clue on how to deal with the situation. But every time he sinned against me, he would assure me that he loved me. I felt devastated, broken, and alone.

The older I got, the more that I craved for the love of a mother and a father. Since my mother was a whole country away, I clung to my father, hoping that one day he would become the father I needed. I lived to please him. I would die if anything harmed him. I put him before God and I put him before myself. He had such a powerful presence that I felt overpowered by him.

One day, I felt like I was reaching the last straw; I could not continue living like this. I called on death, but death was nowhere to be found. The pain was like no pain I had ever experienced before. Something inside me cried and yelled "Save me, Oh Lord. I cannot do it alone."

God did save me, but it would take years before I realized that. The problems heaped onto me like a mountain. The tears kept dropping from my eyes. I did not know much about God.

As a matter of fact, I didn't know much about myself. God separated my father and me. He took him away from me. It was painful, excruciatingly painful. Nonetheless, it was through this pain that He rescued me and finally gave me peace.

I am using my own story to make a point: God is the only savior! Every time we turn a human being (ourselves or another person) or an object into a divinity, we are committing idolatry. In Exodus 20:3 God clearly says: "You should not have any other God but me." We can be sure when we expect from a man to be or act as God, he will fall flat on his face. Yes, God uses people to help us in every circumstance. However, they are not meant to take His place. He is the one who started the good work in you and He will be sure to complete it, just as stated in Philippians 1:6.

I can hear you say: "It's not fair. A child expects her parents to love her. What could be wrong with that?" There is nothing wrong with that. You are absolutely right. As a child, I desperately sought my parents' love.

But when I got older, I realized that my parents were incapable of showing me parental love simply because they were not submissive to the ways of God. If I keep insisting that they should have shown me love for me to be whole, then I am fooling myself.

Only God can make me whole. If I put them in the place of God s, then they would surely fail and feel frustrated.

We are kept away from God and the redemption that His love brings by a multitude of factors. Our past can intrude upon us causing us to waste time and strength. We believe that any of a countless number of different probable paths is possible, and we are sold this lie on a daily basis.

Because God has not helped us in the past, we might feel that we cannot be saved and that we are lost to Him. That is when we start to think that He will not hear our call. We are dissuaded even from trying to reach out and to make Him hear our desperate voices. We don't have the courage to ask Him for help, and that is one of the biggest errors we could make.

But God does not work like this. God is waiting for you! It does not matter to Him how long you have been away and how far you believe you have strayed yourself from His path. You can turn around today and God will be waiting for you, ready to welcome you back into the light. What other savior offers this? Is there anything more truly wonderful than the unconditional love that God grants all his children?

God knows that his creations are flawed, but he gave us free will to let us to choose to return. We can wander and be lost in the spiritual wilderness for many years desperately seeking for an alternative, but eventually, each false idol will only lead to further disappointment.

Like me, there are many of you who are desperately looking for the love, care or attention of someone who is not willing or who is not capable of loving us the way God intended us to be loved.

That is the moment when you feel you will never have it all or that you will never be a complete person until you finally get it. You are constantly seeking to be rescued. The problem is that humans get tired. They wear out. Some people will really try to help you.

Others will not even look your way. But God is here for the long haul. He is here to rescue you and to be your savior for your entire lifetime. First Corinthians 1:10 states: "And He did rescue us from mortal danger, and He will rescue us again. We have placed our confidence in Him, and He will continue to rescue us."

Don't place yourself or others as a savior when someone else or you are in trouble. God is the only savior and He is here for you in the good times and in the bad times. Search for Him by studying His word. Pray for deliverance. Cry out to Him. Scriptures show that God is waiting to hear your cry of repentance. He wants to hear your cry because when He comes; you will surely know that it is Him. As Isaiah 43:11 says: "I, yes, I am the Lord, and there is no other Savior. Cling to your savior and He will give you the rest.

Quote to Ponder:

God uses people to help us in every

circumstance. However, they are not

meant to take His place.

Chapter Notes

_____

_____

_____

_____

_____

_____

_____

_____

_____

_____

_____

_____

_____

_____

_____

_____

_____

_____

_____

_____

_____

_____

_____

Work It Out

Memorize:

Isaiah 43:11

"I, yes, I am the Lord, and there is no other Savior. Cling to your savior and He will give you the rest."

Journal:

Prompt:

How have you given the role of savior to people or things in your life? Have they been able to carry out that awesome responsibility?

Pray:

Lord, please reveal to me where I have made others savior over you, amen.

Chapter 11

Chosen to Bear Fruit

"You did not choose me,
but I chose you and appointed you to go
and bear fruit-fruit that will last.
Then the Father will give you whatever you ask
in my name."
John 15:16 (NIV)

There are so many people who are being invaded by their pasts, which Satan uses as the accuser that keeps tormenting and reminding them of every occasion when they failed. This happens because Satan desperately wants them to remain in their brokenness.

When that happens, we experience feelings of absolute worthlessness. We feel as if we have no personal value at all. Some of us may feel dirty and damaged. Satan wants us to believe we are terrible people who should live in isolation and that we will never be forgiven.

But how can we have no value when Jesus chose us? How can we have no value when God created us after His own image? There's no doubt that sin has distorted that image. But when Jesus died on the cross, He freed us from the slavery of sin. We became slaves of righteousness. He encouraged us to go and produce lasting fruit. God has chosen you for greatness. Don't ever allow Satan to lie to you again.

Satan has a plan for you. He knows your weaknesses and how to exploit them for his own benefit and for his own purposes. Satan has been watching you as you move away from God. He knows that if you return to God, he will no longer be able to exert power over you and use you as one of his agents on Earth. Satan does not want to give up that power and will use whatever means he can to keep you in his thrall.

We must remember that God himself cast Satan out of heaven and, therefore, He knows what riches and rewards are waiting for those who can pass through the heavenly gates. As he cannot enter himself, he does it all to keep you from doing so too, because if you do so, he knows you will forever be out of his reach. So, what does he do? He permanently tries to win your soul and he does it using any mean, through any trick in the book and through many more that we ignore.

God has created you as an ever-lasting fruit. However, depravity craves innocence. Satan wants to corrupt your soul and keep you away from living in the eternal light. By recognizing the lies, smoke and mirrors Satan uses, you can reject his advances and keep him from influencing your life. If you see the tricks and temptations for what they truly are then you can arm yourself and fight them back.

Jesus has chosen you and He can give you all you need to reject Satan. The tools are probably already within your grasp but you may have not found that out yet. Do you own a Bible? Do you have access to online Holy Scriptures? You can use this knowledge to defend yourself against the damaging intrusions from your past and from the malicious temptations presented by Satan.

By reading the scriptures on a daily basis and by doing it in an active way, you can begin to tread the path to become a conqueror. To read in an active, way all you need is a pen in your hand and a question in your mind. Do not be afraid to mark in your Bible; your markings will serve as reminders of your path and how much you have grown.

Applying yourself to study the Bible in this manner has many advantages. If you are committed to read the full Bible, keeping notes you will help you to retain more information. If you simply read page after page, you will probably lose a big percentage of the valuable wisdom and truth contained within those pages.

Always try to take notes so that you can refer back to passages that may later be especially relevant to you, depending on the situation you may be going through. If you keep notes, you will retain the information more easily. Keep notes and any passages you are unsure about can be revisited at a later moment either in the company of others such a spiritual leader, in a study group or just in solitude searching for answers.

Your notes will become a record of your personal journey on the path and into the light. God wants each of His creations to return to Him but, since He gave us free will, only each individual can choose to take that first step. Once the choice is made, you will truly start to feel the benefits as light begins to enter your life and the Lord starts to work through you. No longer will Satan be able to trick you. With the light shining upon you, shadows will be cast away.

The beauty of God's design will be revealed and you will no longer have to fear. Taking these steps is a simple process. You only have to surrender and accept putting Him in control. Once you acknowledge God as the true Lord and give up to personal control, you will be able to embark on this enlightening path.

What once seemed nebulous will now be revealed in holy light. The understanding that was denied to you will become clear now. This is all possible only with that simple first step, taking that step must be done with a sincere and open heart.

Turning your back on Satan is what will let God's light shine through you. You will be able to realize your greatness with your newly empowered self. Liberating yourself from your distorted self-image will allow you to repel intrusions from the incisive past and be freed from the slavery of sin. This will allow your fruit to bloom nourished by the Lord.

Negative thought cycles try to keep us enslaved but with the scriptures and the light of the Lord, we can all be free. If you are tired of repeating the same mistakes, want to break free and walk the path towards becoming a conqueror, all you have to do is to make the decision and take these first steps. God has been waiting for you to return to his arms.

Quote to Ponder:

"If you see the tricks and temptations

for what they truly are then you can

arm yourself and fight them back."

Chapter Notes

Work It Out

Memorize:

John 15:16

"You did not choose me, but I chose you and appointed you to go and bear fruit-fruit that will last. Then the Father will give you whatever you ask in my name."

Journal:

Prompt:

In what ways you have been fruitful and in what areas of your life can you improve?

Pray:

Lord, help me to bear fruits that are pleasing to you. Amen.

Chapter 12

The Word That Heals

"He sent out His word
and healed them,
snatching them from the door of death."
Psalm 107:20

I did not know how to deal with the effects of abuse. I was constantly at the death's door; attempting suicide was so appealing to me. When I was not successful in anything I did, I would become my own judge and tell God how He should punish me.

If He would not terminate my life, then He had my permission to inflict me even more pain by keeping me in the prison of my own mind, by not allowing me to experience the love of a husband, by not allowing me to know what it's like to raise a family. I was convinced that I did not deserve anything good, and I was not shy to tell Him so.

Little did I know that no one tells God what to do. Even though I wanted death so badly, God always found a way to remind me that what I was doing was wrong. He saved me from the passing through the doors of death more times than I can remember. His Word saved me because He had a plan for me.

Do you think there is no hope for you? How can you keep your past from invading your present and destroying your future? Do you think your brokenness will never be healed? Crying out to the Lord and heeding His word can heal you.

In Psalm 107, we read about people who are destroyed in every sense of the word. They have experienced all kinds of trouble: homelessness, hunger, prison, rebellion, and addictions, to mention just a few. "Then they cried out to the Lord in their trouble; He saved them out of their distresses" (Psalm 107:13).

He is ready to do the same for you too! God is ready to save you no matter how big your troubles are. He is especially loving and helpful to the brokenhearted. God's Words are spirit and life. (John 6:63).

In (2 Timothy 3:16-17) we learn that:

> All scripture is inspired by God and is useful to teach us what is true and to make us realize what is wrong in our lives. It corrects us when we are wrong and teaches us to do what is right. God uses it to prepare and equip his people to do every good work.

Are you ready to be healed? Are you ready to allow His spirit to guide you out of the darkness? Then take the Word of God and apply it to your life! It is the medicine you necessitate to be cured and saved!

It is by the Word of God that you should measure everything in your life. It will teach you to distinguish the truth from the lies. It will open your eyes and you will be able to become aware of your sins and it will show you the right way to live. It will show you how to live so as to please God. It will prepare and equip you to carry out God's plan for your life.

The Word of God will enable you to "live as a real conqueror".

However, you must believe. Healing can be yours only if you sincerely believe and obey the Word of God. His name is Jehovah-Raphael, the God who heals. There is no hurt that he cannot heal.

There is nothing broken that he cannot restore. You cannot do it on your own. As Mathew 4:4 states: "People do not live by bread alone, but on every word that comes from the mouth of God."

We are blessed to live during this moment in time. We have no shortage of Bibles. The Bible is easily accessible to anyone willing to learn His Word.

You can find the Bible practically in every language, dialect and style. You can find Bibles in bookstores, libraries, hotel rooms, and on bookshelves or bedside tables at family homes, to mention just a few.

In the past, only priests had the privilege of reading the Bible. However, things have changed for good over time and nowadays we all have access to the Word of God.

We have no excuse to be spiritually starving and suffering from all sorts of spiritual, emotional and psychosomatic diseases.

God's medicine is here.

The medicine is available to anyone willing to take it and heal. The question is: Are you really willing to take it? Are you determined to be healed? Can you make that commitment with yourself?

The following are ways to make the Bible a part of your daily life:

Accept the inspiration and the authority of the Bible

Make this the foundation for your walk with Christ. I have seen many people read the Bible; it did nothing for them because they did not believe what they were reading. I used to be like them long time ago. . I was so focused on my brokenness; I did not believe the Word of God.

I spent most of my life going to church and hearing about God, but until I really believed—the Word had no effect on me. Now it is your time to make the decision. Decide right now to let the Bible be the guiding authority of your life. Let the Bible be the law ruling your life.

Whenever you need to make decisions; whenever you have to solve a problem; whenever you need correction and encouragement; whenever you may need to find relief—you will be able to rely on the Bible to guide you to enlightenment.

Many times we get into trouble because we listen to the wrong counselors. We listen to ungodly friends. We listen to what our culture dictates or to what the society qualifies as convenient. We listen to the television. We listen to our confused feelings.

We want things to make sense and to be logical. Let me inform you that all those things are flawed and cannot be trusted. It is up to you to decide to let the Word of God be the guiding light that will lead you away from the darkness.

Once you make the decision, you must remain strong on your faith and let God's Word rule your life, even in those moments when things may seem not to make sense to you.

Study and Learn the Word of God

Once we've accepted that the Word of God is the only authoritative standard in our lives, we must study it. We have to be receptive to the Word of God in order to bear fruit. When we are being receptive, we are ensuring that the Word of God will grow as a root within our souls.

So make it a priority to read the Bible daily! Cut down the time you waste on the telephone, watching television, and surfing on the Internet and spend it reading the Bible. Take up the challenge to read the entire Bible by using a Bible reading plan.

Dig deeper in your studies by asking questions. Write your thoughts down in a journal or notepad or right there in your Bible.

James 1:25 states; "But if you look carefully into the perfect law that sets you free, and if you do what it says and don't forget what you heard, then God will bless you for doing it."

God does not only want us to read and study the texts of the Bible, He wants us to remember them. It is not just about reading and memorizing them in a mechanical manner, it is about understanding and comprehending them.

When you remember the Word of God you can use it as a shield to resist the Devil and his malicious schemes. Escape from his evil agenda with the Word of God. Study and learn His word with determination and commitment.

Once you have learned it, you will be able to recall verses just in the nick of time, you will find answers and alleviating words in those crucial times when you need a good advice or when you have to make a vital decision or simply to give comfort to your soul in moments of sorrow.

As we remember and meditate on the Word of God, we become more like Christ.

Our brokenness becomes a thing of the past. That does not mean we will never feel pain again. It does mean that will be prepared to deal with pain in a godly manner.

The Word of God will not prevent us from being hurt or feeling pain, but it will teach us to deal with it wisely and hopefully.

Put What You Have Learned into Practice

It is easy to read the Word of God. What is not so easy is to practice it though. The difficulty resides in applying that wisdom into our lives and doing what the Word says. We must obey the Word, otherwise it will be useless.

There is no sense in reading the Word but not following it. Besides, we will never find a better counselor, better advice, than the one given by God through His Word. Hebrews 13:7 states: "Everyone who hears these words of mine and puts them into practice is like a wise man who built his house on the rock."

Practicing the Word of God is hard because we don't like changes, we tend to leave things as they are since we are afraid of the unknown we want to stay in our comfort zone even though it is invading our present and destroying our future.

Nonetheless, the Word of God seeks to renew us. God wants to heal our wounds. God wants to heal our brokenness and alleviate our pain. Therefore, major adjustments and changes will be required. You may find it necessary to develop a plan of action by writing down exactly what you intend to do, how you will do it, and by when you will do it.

Make it a habit to read over your plan regularly, preferably at morning, afternoon, and night. Otherwise, it may enter from one ear and get out of your mind from the other one.

God is ready to heal and save you! He has snatched you right from the door of death, if not, you would not be reading this book right now. His Word has everything you need to heal your brokenness and win the war that is being fought within yourself.

Yes, your spirit may be a battlefield in which darkness and light are fighting against each other. But you have what it takes to take you to the light, you have the Word. Let the Word become the sword that will liberate your soul.

Quote to Ponder:

"Once you make the decision, you must remain strong on your faith and let God's Word rule your life, even in those moments when things may seem not to make sense to you."

Chapter Notes

_____

_____

_____

_____

_____

_____

_____

_____

_____

_____

_____

_____

_____

_____

_____

_____

_____

_____

_____

_____

_____

_____

_____

<u>Work It Out</u>

Memorize:

2 Timothy 3:16-17

"All scripture is inspired by God and is useful to teach us what is true and to make us realize what is wrong in our lives. It corrects us when we are wrong and teaches us to do what is right. God uses it to prepare and equip his people to do every good work."

Journal:

Prompt:

Do you have a daily bible reading plan? If not, you can easily get one by going online or purchasing a bible. There is usually a plan in the back of most bibles. What and how has the Word of God teach you?

Pray: Thank you Lord for your Word. Help me use it to be more than a conqueror. Amen.

Chapter 13

You Are Who God Says You Are"

"Jesus...says, 'Let go of your complaints,
forgive those who loved you poorly,
step over your feelings of being rejected,
and have the courage to trust
that you won't fall into an abyss
of nothingness but into the safe embrace
of a God whose love will heal all your
wounds."

— Henri J.M. Nouwen
Here and Now: Living in the Spirit

The Problem of Identity

Who are you? That is one of the most
fundamental questions you should find an answer
to. In my experience as an educator, speaker, author

and life coach, I constantly come across thousands of people who suffer from the "identity problem".

They tend to define their lives by their pasts, rather than defining themselves as individuals with a past, which is a very different thing. For example, Rebecca came to me after a presentation to ask me a question. However, she found it necessary to tell me that she had grown up in a dysfunctional family and suffered from low self-esteem as a consequence of her past life.

Some other people, when asked who they are, immediately answer to that question telling what they do for a living. For example, "I am an educator", or "I am a nurse." There are others who reply mentioning a role they play in life, for instance, "I am a mother"," I am a wife" or "I am a student".

Do you actually think that those types of answers mentioned above truly answer the question that is being asked? We must admit that there are still so many people that have absolutely no idea how to answer to the question: Who are you? Now, what about you? Are you among them? Do you know who you really are?

One reason why many people allow the identity problem to continue invading their lives is that, it is a twisted way of finding some value in themselves. They think that defining their lives by their pasts make them important. Another reason is that it gives them a sense of belonging.

That is the reason why there are so many different support groups and programs which are tailored for every negative experience imaginable. However, instead of using them as a stepping-stone to move to a better place, people tend to linger in the group longer than necessary because they are in desperate need of companion and understanding.

We feel so comfortable with the continuous love, acceptance, compassion, or whatever it may be that suits our emotional needs—that it is almost impossible to move forward. What happens it that we are precisely being invaded by our pasts. We have become too comfortable with our brokenness that we carry around it as a badge.

We think that if we take that badge off and put it away, we will not be loved or get the attention we need. We are not finding any values within ourselves, we don't think we deserve being loved for ourselves, and we think we have nothing worthy in us to capture the attention, compassion and affection of the others, so we recur to our past.

You are experiencing identity problems because you don't understand that apart from God, you have no identity. The identity problem was the biggest problem I had to face. It seemed to me that everything I said, thought, or did was wrong.

I had a problem with everything.

It was much later when I realized that I was constantly thinking, talking or doing something against myself. Although it was extremely negative, however, the focus was on me. But if the focus is on me, it cannot be on God.

Receive Jesus as Your Personal Savior

You are who God says you are when you accept Jesus Christ as your personal savior. As 2 Corinthians 5:17 states: "This means that anyone who belongs to Christ has become a new person. The old life is gone, and a new life has begun." Isn't that magnificent?

Meditate on the Word of God

For the point of being who God says you are to be ingrained in your head and in your heart, you must meditate on who He says you are. So read your Bible for at least 15 minutes per day and liberally mark in your Bible areas where he speaks to you.

Try this, take God at His word and agree with Him. He never lies, so His word is the truth. Believe that

- ✓ You are complete in Him *(Colossians 2:10)*
- ✓ You can do all things *(Philippians 4:13)*.
- ✓ You are more than a conqueror (*Romans 8:37).*
- ✓ You are an overcomer *(Revelation 12:11)*
- ✓ You are God's masterpiece *(Ephesians 2:10).*
- ✓ You are God's child *(1Peter 1:23).*

- ✓ You are the light of the world *(Mathew 5:14)*
- ✓ You are forgiven *(Ephesians 1:7)*.
- ✓ You are delivered *(Colossians 1:13)*.
- ✓ You are loved *(Romans 1:7)*.

Claim these Scriptures and make them your own. Let's partner with God to create the life he has always destined for you and become the conqueror that you are.

Quote to Ponder:

"You are who God says you are when you accept Jesus Christ as your personal savior."

<u>Chapter Notes</u>

Work It Out

Memorize:

Ephesians 2:10

"You are God's masterpiece."

Journal:

Prompt:

Take a moment and research 10 new beautiful things that God has said about you. Write the verses here.

Pray:

Lord, help me to understand the depth of your love for me. Help me to see myself as you see me, amen.

Chapter 14

Override Your Operating System

"…whatever is true, whatever is noble,
whatever is right, whatever is pure,
whatever is lovely, whatever is admirable—
if anything is excellent or praiseworthy—
think about such things."

Philippians 4:8

Everything in your life starts with a thought. Those thoughts can be either productive or destructive thoughts. People who allow themselves to be invaded by the past are those who practice what I call "destructive thinking". They constantly use the past against themselves rather than for themselves.

I remember being stuck in that mindset myself. For example, I was sexually abused by my father as a child. As a result, I developed this negative mindset about how damaged I was and how I was disgusting as a person. I thought of myself as a coward. I would go over and over in my mind thinking about how I could have avoided such situation. And, I believed that if I could not have avoided the situation, at least I could have come out of it earlier. I punished myself up to the point of trying to commit suicide. That was destructive thinking.

I overcame this mindset by monitoring my thoughts. It was not easy, it required quite a mental effort trying to gain control of my own thoughts and emotions. I came up with a list of things that were productive, nurturing or positive for me to think about.

If my thoughts were not productive or fell into the categories in this list below, I would recognize them right away, and replace the destructive thought with more pleasant and productive ones. Below is the list I came up with.

When prompted to think about...I thought about... I felt...

Hate	Love	Loved
Ugliness	Beauty	Beautiful
Powerlessness	Power	Powerful
Weakness	Strength	Strong
Division/Revenge	Peace	Peaceful
Impatience	Patience	Patient
Bondage	Freedom	Free

You can do the same thing. Be conscious of what you are thinking of. Determine whether or not the thoughts you are thinking are helping you to become a better person, a better neighbor, a better mother, a better wife, or a better business leader.

If they are not doing anything good in your life, replace them. You may want to customize the list mentioned above to your own needs. Start by writing down your predominant thoughts, then find a better alternative to each thought, and write it in the first person, present tense.

Is Your Mind Too Busy?

Having an overactive mind is another indicator that tells you are being invaded. That is when you allow your mind to take up many thoughts at a time. That occurs because you are avoiding the real problem. You are hiding the real problem behind that confusing net of thoughts.

As you know thoughts lead to actions, therefore, people whose minds are too busy tend to load up their schedules with things that have nothing to do with their real purpose or mission in life. They are too busy having conversations in their minds and with their minds, that they confuse business thinking with productivity.

They convince themselves that they are doing something productive when in reality they are doing nothing... They give themselves so much things to think about that they cannot hear the still small voice inside them urging them to take a rest.

When you leave yourself no room for inspiration, you are being invaded. When you are being invaded by your past, the right approaches to a better life can be in front of you and you can be missing them; you will crawl back to the destructive nature of your past because your mind is too busy to recognize it.

Do You Often Wander and Wonder?

If you have a wandering-wondering mind, you are most likely being invaded. A wandering mind is a mind that is unable to concentrate on specific a thing for a certain length of time. That is a direct result of having allowed the mind to do whatever it wants whenever it wants to do it.

For example, you may have a great business idea that you know will succeed if you devote your time and efforts to it. When a friend talks about opening a restaurant, all of a sudden you want to open a restaurant. Then you hear on the radio that a landscaping business is always a good business to start. So now, you also want to start a landscaping business. Then, your church talks about an opportunity to head up a new ministry. That sounds interesting to you too. Allowing your mind to roam aimlessly will keep producing more of the same results.

Another example that can help to emphasize the point that I am trying to communicate, is when one is engaged in conversation. Imagine your husband is talking to you about spending quality time with the children. While he is talking, you are thinking about all the things that you meant to do today but you did not get to do.

In the meantime, you do not hear a word what your husband is saying. If you are honest, you should ask him to repeat what he has just said because you were not paying attention. But what the majority of the people do, is acting as if they have heard everything.

To resolve that problem, you have to make an effort to remain in the present. Work on improving your listening skills while making eye contact with the person you are having a conversation with.

To help your mind stay focused, procure the help of motivational and inspirational tapes and CDs. Listen to them on a daily basis so as to train your mind to stay focused on the current issues or tasks.

Do You Frequently Wonder?

Do you often find yourself saying…?

"I wonder what would happen if I had a degree."

"I wonder what he would think of me if he knew about my past."

"I wonder what could happen if I get this job."

A person who wonders excessively is a person that has a doubtful mind. People who have doubtful minds are not sure about anything. That was me in my college years.

I was known for changing majors at least once a semester. I wondered what it would be like to be a nurse, a doctor, a singer, a dancer, an actress or an accountant…and the list went on. In the midst of wondering, I exhausted myself.

If you are always wondering about everything under the sun, the only positive alternative is to take action. Decide to take definitive steps to get what you are wondering about.

For example, getting a higher degree requires researching universities, filling out admission applications, applying for financial aid, and taking entrance exams. Getting into action is empowering. . A wondering mind leads to indecision, doubt, and confusion. All those feelings leave you extremely tired and with no energy to do anything really productive.

Are You Often in State of Confusion?

If you find yourself in a state of mental confusion, more than likely you are being invaded by your past. You know you are being invaded when you are uncertain about anything and everything that you are doing.

Your main concern is answering "why." You look for the logic in everything. You go around and around until you find yourself dizzy with confusion. Therefore, you remain stagnant and unable to make and/or follow your decisions.

At times you know something is wrong but you allow confusion to lead you the opposite way. The reverse is also true. You must understand that you may never be able to find the "why" behind every single thing you do.

Are You Often Double-minded?

Doubts lead to double-mindedness. That is when you waver from one thing to another. One of my coaching clients came to me one day feeling very discouraged. She wanted to overcome the issues of her past but she found herself invaded by frequent thoughts of doubt.

She was in a coaching program, listening to inspirational CDs, praying, and saying her affirmations; however, she still felt in her mind that she would never be able to succeed.

I immediately recognized her situation as a case of double-mindedness, a case of doubt. She doubted whether or not she could ever have a life different from the one she lived in her past.

Many people repeatedly go through this cycle over and over during their lives. Essentially, they allow a double mind to set the pace. In reality, there is no pace. They are stuck, you are stuck. You will continue to be stuck until you believe that what you are seeking for is possible and until you believe wholeheartedly that you can achieve it.

Are You Often Worried and Anxious?

Invasion from your past may also come through worry and anxiety. If you find yourself constantly worrying about everything and anything, you may be an addict. When you don't have things to worry about, you seem to be seeking for concerns.

You don't have real problems but you invent them in your mind. I consider this an attack because as long as you keep remaining anxious and worried, you will never achieve your potential.

Do You Find It Difficult to Control Your Emotions?

If you find that you cannot control your emotions as a result of what happened to you in your past, you are being invaded. Are you often angry for no apparent reason? Are you resentful? Do you fear taking risks? One man once told me, "I am always angry because I was a great husband and my wife still left me."

If you find that your emotions are controlling you, instead of the other way around, then that is an issue that needs to be addressed.

Are You Fearful?

When we are afraid about burglars breaking in our homes, we order a security system to be installed. To keep bugs from destroying our lawn, we order lawn service. To get rid of a headache, we take painkillers.

These are three examples of how we control the situations in our lives. Control usually comes into the picture when we fear something. Whenever fear rears its ugly head, we want to be God instead of calling on God.

I remember one of the ways in which my past used to invade my present was through the constant thought that I was not good enough. I kept thinking that if people knew what had happened to me in the past, they would never look at me in the same way again.

So, I pretended to be a person who had it all together. I acted as this self-sufficient person who could do everything for herself and by herself. I was my own "god" because my focus was always on me, what happened to me, and how to hide it from others.

The problem with living a permanent lie is that one day something will go wrong. Sooner or later our brokenness will emerge and the invasion will continue. We cannot be strong all the time. We cannot pretend to be right and all the time. Apostle Paul experienced the same thing.

In Romans 7:15-17 he says: If we want our lives to change, if we want the past to stop invading our present and destroying our future, we have to be honest with God, others, and ourselves. Fear is an energy zapper. It will leave you weak, exhausted, and hopeless.

The one and only real way to get rid of the slavery of our own past is to turn to God, hear His word, learn His Word, and follow Him. He will be the only guide to take us out of the tunnel of darkness and take us to the light.

Quote to Ponder:

"When you leave yourself no room for inspiration, you are being invaded."

Chapter Notes

_____

_____

_____

_____

_____

_____

_____

_____

_____

_____

_____

_____

_____

_____

_____

_____

_____

_____

_____

_____

_____

_____

_____

Work It Out

Memorize:

Philippians 4:8

"...whatever is true, whatever is noble, whatever is right, whatever is pure, whatever is lovely, whatever is admirable—if anything is excellent or praiseworthy—think about such things."

Journal:

Prompt:

Make a list of noble, right, pure, lovely, admirable things you can think about today.

Pray:

Lord, help me see all the noble, right, pure, lovely, and admirable things to think about today. Amen.

Chapter 15

You Are More than Conquerors

What, then, shall we say
in response to these things?
If God is for us, who can be against us?
Who shall separate us from the love of Christ?
Shall trouble or hardship
or persecution or famine
or nakedness or danger or sword?
No, in all these things
we are more than conquerors
through him who loved us

Romans 8:31-39

It is impossible to prevent other people from disappointing you. It is not under your control. In the past, you may have had experiences that were outside of yourself. To stop your past from invading your present and destroying your future, you must deal with your very personal internal forces—where you are in total control. When you recognize you hold the key, you are on your way to becoming a conqueror. God has already spoken; it is up to you to take the step of faith.

Here are some steps you can take to help your transition from a victim to a conqueror:

Acknowledge You Are the Problem

It may be hard for you to acknowledge you are the one with the problem. I know that may be hard to swallow but it is essential to success and for you to become a conqueror. You may have suffered terrible and demeaning circumstances in your past, but those things do not have any control over you unless you give them control.

The best thing you can do with your past experiences is to learn from them. Your past is a great resource you can use to create the life you want. It is not a tool to use to keep you paralyzed and in a destructive mode. If you are using your past in such a manner, it means you have replaced those who have hurt you in the past.

Since it is an internal battle, only you can decide to fight it. You have to realize you own the problem before finding a solution.

This is excellent news. It is empowering. While you may not able to control other people and their behaviors you are in the position to control your actions and behaviors. It's up to you to make the choice.

Keep Moving Forward

On your way to become a conqueror, it is essential to understand that your past experiences will never go away, they just won't vanish. They are parts of you for life that are here to stay, even when they seemed to have momentarily disappeared.

Therefore, you will find yourself in situations where you will be reminded of your past. When they come, you must keep moving forward despite the pains and the fears.

When your past is invading your present and destroying your future, you may think you need to eliminate every trace of the past to live a successful life. That could not be more distant from the truth. You must endure until the end, reprogramming your mind and creating positive experiences to kick off the negative experiences that keep you stuck.

You shall try to create positive experiences through meaningful relationships. Your negative experiences will become dim in comparison.

Accept People for Who They Are

To stop your past from invading your present and destroying your future, you must accept people for who they are, not for what you want them to be. Take Sean for example: when he was growing up, his father was never home. He would pop up whenever it was convenient for him.

Somehow, Sean interpreted his father's absence as if it meant that he was an unlovable kid and, therefore his father did not want to be a part of his life. As time went by, and Sean reached adulthood, he kept working hard to get his father's approval. He was disappointed every now and then. As you may deduct, Sean's father didn't know how to be a father and, over the years, he had shown no sign that he really wanted to become a good father.

If Sean continued expecting father and son bonding actions or attitudes from his father, he would have continued to be stuck in the repeating the cycle of hurt and disappointment.

Let It Go

Gary has been divorced for more than ten years, and he still resents his ex-wife because he thinks she is responsible for his current situation in life. When they were married, the couple used to do everything together. They ran the house and the family business together as a team. It was the perfect life for Gary. But now he feels miserable and unproductive. How could she do this to him?

That's the question Gary continues to ask himself every time he thinks about how his life has deteriorated since they divorced. He is afraid to start any new relationship—romantic, business, or any other kind of relationship that may involve emotions or expectations. He thinks he won't be able to be happy again.

There are so many individuals like Gary out there. The pain they suffered in the past, may be years ago, keeps them engaged as if it was happening in the present. Somehow, their past keeps them paralyzed and prevents them from moving forward.

Becoming a conqueror requires you to stop this cycle. Let it go. Give it up. Move on. Understand that I am not minimizing or demeaning your pain and the damage that has been done to you. I have been hurt too, so I understand exactly how you feel.

However, the more attention you give to your pain, the more it will continue to grow. Your mind is not capable of comprehending an unlimited number of problems and being successful at finding solutions for all of them at the same time.

Your mind can handle just a few issues at a time. Giving too much attention to the pains of your past, will suffocate any chances you may have to create a future totally different from your past.

Therefore, spend your time on activities that nurture, nourish, improve, and elevate your current state of mind and being. You might want to do things such as taking a walk in a beautiful park or on the beach, playing with your kids, reading to them, or going back to school and learning something new, for example.

Be creative and have fun! Dedicate your time and efforts to people and activities that help you become a better person. Then, after you do so, you will discover that you have finally created a brand new life.

Keep looking towards the future. Take action each day to take a step forward. Take special care of yourself. Only after you learn how to take good care of yourself, you will be able to effectively take care of others. If you have a family, take care of your family. My family helped to save my life. I focused more on taking care of them than dwelling on my hurts and pains.

When you are only concerned about your pain, you are inadvertently hurting those who care about you. You are telling them your pain is more important than them. You want them to feel sorry for you. This type of behavior is selfish and keeps you in the same vicious cycle, so let it go. Give your energy to develop your potential and to love unconditionally.

Replace Bad Habits with Good Habits

When the past has invaded your thoughts, behaviors, and actions, it is most likely that those habits you've been having are actually bad habits. Dwelling in the past does not contribute to learning and acquiring good habits. When we keep doing prejudicial things, we are asking the world to reinforce the habits that are destroying our future.

One example of that, is when you go around expecting negative outcomes every time you try something new. Interestingly enough, life is funny that way. It will give you what you expect to happen.

To introduce some new habits into your life, you have to be able to challenge yourself. Ask yourself, "Am I making this decision based on my past? What do I do on a daily basis to sabotage my mission in life? Do I put everybody in a box or do I see people as individuals?"

As a person who is being invaded by the past, here are a few examples on how to change your habits. If you are a complainer, become a problem solver. If you make excuses, take responsibility for your life.

If you are a negative person, take the necessary steps to become a positive person. It does not matter how bad your habits are, you can turn them around by working on them on a daily basis. It has been said that it takes about twenty-one days to change a habit. All you have to do is keep working on it and it will become a natural thing to you.

For example, if you start waking up at the same hour every day by an alarm clock, as time goes by, you will continue to wake up at the same time even without an alarm clock. Over time, you will adjust to it and start doing it automatically.

Of course, that does not mean you will not experience any pain and discomfort. You will, because you are not used to it. But pain and discomfort are better than giving up on your life and letting your past take over you. You must constantly seek to ameliorate your life. You must constantly challenge your habits and behaviors in order to be able to take advantage of the opportunities surrounding you.

Step Outside Your Box and Help Someone

Too many times, when we are being invaded by our pasts and the future seems forever unclear, we tend to make everything go around ourselves. "I need someone to take care of me. I am always the center of attention. I must buy everything I see because I deserve it."

That is pure selfishness. The problem with dwelling in the past is that we are always taking more than we are giving. That becomes a problem because we overextend those who care, tolerate, and love us.

What we ought to be doing is shaking things up in our lives. Choose to have a good life. Choose to surround yourself with people who can help make good things happen. Engage yourself in activities that contribute to create that good life that you desire on a daily basis.

Invest in yourself by taking the time to educate yourself and care for yourself. In essence, create a life completely different from that past that includes everything you mistakenly have been holding on to, and integrate to your new life everything you consider dear. It will not happen in a day, but that is better than remaining in the past and letting it control any possible chances of having a good life.

Another thing we ought to do in order to shake things up is stepping out of the box and helping someone, mentor someone. That may sound shivery because many of us think we have nothing worthwhile to share or give. I beg to differ. We have so much to share.

When you were fighting this battle of the past, you encountered angels on your path: those who were willing to give you a smile or a comforting hug, those who told you everything would turn out for good. You had people who believed in you and people who showed you the way when you were lost. You may call them friends, teachers, pastors, counselors, coaches, or mentors.

Furthermore, they may have even been absolute strangers or even the deceased. Wait and keep reading before you say that I'm crazy; let me explain what I mean. Some of the best mentors I have found were found within the pages of the books I read.

Many of those books that I read were autobiographies. I have learned from other people's lives. Reading autobiographies allowed me to know that someone else had previously traveled along a similar path and their autobiographies told me how they were able to deal with it.

When you help someone by dedicating some of your time to that person, it brings more significance to both, you and that the person in need of help, affection, guidance or relief. First, you will find out that you are not the only one who is facing hard situations or dealing with problems. Secondly, you will stretch yourself to help find solutions to solve other people's problems. Thirdly, you will give yourself an opportunity to focus on another person and stop being so self-centered. Fourthly, you will impact on someone's life in ways you may never comprehend.

Quote to Ponder:

"The best thing you can do with your past experiences is to learn from them. Your past is a great resource you can use to create the life you want."

Chapter Notes

_____

_____

_____

_____

_____

_____

_____

_____

_____

_____

_____

_____

_____

_____

_____

_____

_____

_____

_____

_____

_____

_____

_____

_____

Work It Out

Memorize:

Romans 8:31-39

"What, then, shall we say in response to these things? If God is for us, who can be against us? Who shall separate us from the love of Christ? Shall trouble or hardship or persecution or famine or nakedness or danger or sword? ... No, in all these things we are more than conquerors through him who loved us"

Journal:

Prompt:

How are you more than a conqueror? Who will guide you from this day forward to live the abundant life you were promised? What tools will He use to do that?

Pray:

> Thank you Lord for winning the battles that we must fight in keeping the past from invading our present and destroying our future. Amen.

Notes

1. Arthur, Kay (2000). Lord, Heal my Hurts. Waterbrook Press. Colorado Springs, CO.

2. Brown, Brene (2012). Daring Greatly: How the Courage to Be Vulnerable Transforms the Way We Live, Love, Parent, and Lead. Gotham Books. New York, New York.

3. Bryron, Katie and Stephen Mitchell (2002). Loving What Is: Four Questions That Can Change Your Life. New York: Harmony Books.

4. Canfield, Jack (2005). The Success Principle: How to Get from Where You Are to Where You Want to Be. HarperCollins Publishers. New York, New York.

5. Maxwell, John C. (2017). No Limits: Blow the Cap off Your Potential. Center Street. New York, New York.

6. Schlessinger, Laura. (2006). Bad Childhood, Good Life: How to Blossom and Thrive in Spite of an Unhappy Childhood.

HarperCollins Publishers. New York, New York.

7. Sol, Mateo. (208). 23 Signs You're Suffering from a Victim Mentality. www.lonerwolf.com/victim-mentality/

About the Author

Dr. GeGe Jasmin is dedicated to empowering women to be Bravingly Unstoppable by helping them discover their best selves through healing, learning, and growing from setbacks, disappointments, and life changing events. She has vast experiences in business, education, and coaching to equip women in achieving their goals and dreams. She is the owner of multiple organizations, such as Legacy Realty International, where she coaches agents to become successful and provide red carpet customer services to home buyers and sellers.

She is a businesswoman, writer, and educator who balances career, business, and family on a daily basis. She is happily married with six children. She maintains a number of licenses such as the Real Estate Broker and Instructor. Dr. Jasmin holds a Master's Degree in Human Resource Development from Florida International University. Additionally, she earned a Doctor of Education specializing in Organizational Learning and Leadership from Barry University. Follow her blogs at

www.drgege.com,

www.legacyrealtyinternational.com to learn about my current projects.

Legacy Publishing
Imagination at Work

www.ingramcontent.com/pod-product-compliance
Lightning Source LLC
Chambersburg PA
CBHW051821090426
42736CB00011B/1596